Classroom Interaction and Social Learning

The contemporary classroom presents a wealth of opportunities for social interaction amongst pupils, and this has led to an increased interest by teachers and researchers in the social nature of learning.

While classroom interaction can be a valuable tool for learning, it does not necessarily lead to useful learning experiences. In this book, the authors use case studies to highlight the use of new methodologies for studying the content and patterns of children's interactions and show how these contribute to their construction of knowledge. The book is presented in three parts:

- **Studying classroom interaction and learning:** an introduction to and overview of existing research and methodologies; a new method of analysis.
- **Classroom interaction in action:** case studies with several areas of emphasis, including classroom organisation, word processors and multimedia, talk in early years and problem-solving situations.
- **Classroom interaction and learning:** the implications for teachers and teaching are discussed.

Classroom Interaction and Social Learning will appeal to teachers and researchers who have an interest in classroom discourse and learning.

Kristiina Kumpulainen is a Senior Research Fellow of the Academy of Finland. **David Wray** is Professor of Literacy Education at the University of Warwick.

Classroom Interaction and Social Learning

From theory to practice

Edited by Kristiina Kumpulainen
and David Wray

ROUTLEDGE / FALMER
Taylor & Francis Group

London and New York

First published 2002 by RoutledgeFalmer
11 New Fetter Lane, London EC4P 4EE

Simultaneously published in the USA and Canada
by RoutledgeFalmer
29 West 35th Street, New York, NY 10001

RoutledgeFalmer is an imprint of the Taylor & Francis Group

© 2002 Kristiina Kumpulainen and David Wray

Typeset in Sabon by BC Typesetting, Bristol BS31 1NZ
Printed and bound in Great Britain by
Biddles Ltd, Guildford and King's Lynn

British Library Cataloguing in Publication Data
A catalogue record for this book is available from the British Library

Library of Congress Cataloging in Publication Data
Kumpulainen, Kristiina, 1966–
    Classroom interaction and collaborative learning: from theory
to practice/Kristiina Kumpulainen and David Wray.
        p.   cm.
    Includes bibliographical references (p.   ) and index.
    ISBN 0–415–23078–0 (hardcover) – ISBN 0–415–23079–9 (pbk.)
    1. Interaction analysis in education. 2. Social interaction in
children. 3. Group work in education. 4. Learning, Psychology of.
I. Wray, David, 1950– II. Title.

LB1034.K86 2001
370.15′23–dc21   2001040370

ISBN 0–415–23078–0 (hbk)
ISBN 0–415–23079–9 (pbk)

Contents

Tables

Acknowledgements

We wish to thank the Academy of Finland, the Cultural Foundation of Finland and the University of Exeter for their financial support in preparing this book and in conducting the case studies which have increased our understanding of the role of social interaction in learning and instruction and through which our analytical method for studying students' classroom interaction and learning emerged. We are particularly grateful to the following for their insightful ideas and valuable contributions to the data collection, analysis and interpretations of students' classroom interactions in a range of learning situations, and also for their collaboration in the preparation of certain chapters: Georgios Fourlas (chapter 4), Susan Rogers (chapter 6), Sinikka Kaartinen (chapter 7) and Mika Mutanen and Hanna Salovaara (chapter 8).

Introduction

Eemeli: yeah . . . but now we have a problem . . . this is too long . . . so . . . could it . . . should we . . .

Santeri: hey . . . let's move these

Eemeli: yeah, yeah . . . let's move . . . these don't belong . . . wait . . . where could the other triangle fit . . . oh

Santeri: or then . . . wait

Eemeli: hey . . . hey . . . what if one of these triangles is the best

Santeri: you mean these

Eemeli: no these ones . . . look then we could use squares that are equal size . . . try to find squares of this size two more . . . that thirty one . . . okay . . . where . . . twenty . . . this one here . . . look Santeri . . . this one goes here like this and this one here and the whole lot goes like this

Santeri: yeah

Eemeli: so . . . it should be formed out of these

Santeri: wait . . . like this

Eemeli: look . . . it is going to be like this

Santeri: oh yes

Eemeli: it should be formed with these

Santeri: yes it should

In this extract, derived from a geometrical problem-solving task in an elementary classroom, two students are actively involved in negotiating a joint meaning for the task and its solution. The reading of this extract is likely to arouse several questions that many educationalists – both researchers and practitioners – might want to investigate and elaborate. These questions may focus on the quality and nature of the interactions between these two students and how these contribute to their academic learning. They might also centre around the social relationships and expectations between the students and how these might facilitate or hinder the participation of both of them in collaborative problem-solving activity. In addition, teachers and researchers might want to look at the ways in which understanding and learning were represented in the students' language or at the role of physical tools in joint problem solving.

In addition to the interpersonal analyses, this extract could also be located within its broader cultural setting. From this perspective, it would be interesting to investigate how the extract reflects the ways in which the learning situation is constructed, as well as how the tacit norms and practices of the culture of the classroom and of the students shape the moment-by-moment interactions in learning activity.

This brief overview of the potential questions that could guide the investigation of the extract demonstrates that classroom interaction provides a rich source of data that can be approached and studied from a range of perspectives. In fact, in recent years, the meaning of social interaction in mediating and supporting the practice of learning in institutions of education has begun to intrigue educational researchers more and more. This can be gauged by the number of research studies that have explored the ways in which knowledge is socially constructed through classroom discourse (e.g. Edwards, 1993; Lemke, 1990; Mercer, 1995; Wells and Chang-Wells, 1992). Studies have also investigated topics such as:

- teachers' use of discourse strategies to orchestrate classroom interaction and to scaffold students' learning (see e.g. Cazden, 1988; Englert, 1992; Fleer, 1992; Langer and Applebee, 1986; Palincsar, 1986; Palincsar and Brown, 1984; Pylvänäinen, Vasama and Kumpulainen (in press); Wood, 1992);
- students' social interactions during collaborative learning activities and the processes and outcomes of these (see e.g. Barnes and Todd, 1977, 1995; Cowie and van der Aalsvoort, 2000; Dillenbourg, 1999; Littleton and Light, 1999; Mercer and Wegeriff, 1999; Sharan and Shachar, 1988; Teasley, 1995; Webb, Troper and Fall, 1995);
- the discourses of students' home and community lives and the impact of differences in these on their learning across the curriculum (see e.g. Cazden, 1988; Delamont, 1976; Jennings and Green, 1999; Maybin, 1991; Phelan, Davidson and Cao, 1991; Wells, 1987).

From the number of research studies conducted in this field, and from the interest shown by educators across the world in developing their classrooms into interactive communities, it seems that in many contemporary classrooms social interaction is seen as a valuable tool for learning. The reasons for the growing interest in classroom interactions, and, more generally, in the processes of learning inherent in social interaction, reflect a theoretical shift in perspectives on learning and instruction. These have begun to emphasise the social and cultural nature of human learning (Mercer, 2000; Resnick, Levine and Teasley, 1991; Rogoff, 1990). Learning tends to be seen not only as a constructive process that takes place in the mind of the learner but also as a process of meaning-making and enculturation into social practices. According to this line of thinking, there is a pedagogical need to construct spaces in classrooms that invite and support learners' participation in diverse communities of practice, including specific subject domains and their discourses. On the other hand, classrooms need to be spaces that allow for difference by inviting all participants in the learning community to contribute to the ongoing interaction with their own voices and perspectives (Wells, 1999).

Contemporary views of learning and their pedagogical applications, including student-centred learning activities and collaborative working modes, are changing the traditional interaction patterns of many classrooms and affecting the roles of teachers and students as communicators and learners. Such learning situations give students more opportunities to participate, observe, reflect on, and practise socially shared ways of knowing and thinking, and the extended student interactions arising from these environments can be regarded as windows on students' meaning-making and knowledge construction processes. Yet, mere opportunities to participate in social interaction will not necessarily lead to meaningful learning experiences. Consequently, serious attention has to be paid to the patterns and content of students' interactions and how these support or challenge their learning. Moreover, careful attention needs to be paid to the contexts in which social interaction is embedded and how they contribute to or influence learning practices in the classroom.

Several implications arise from this. Firstly, there is a need for a summary review of existing knowledge about classroom interaction and learning that can be used by practitioners and researchers to underpin future work in classroom settings. Secondly, it is clear that wider research is needed in this area and, thirdly, that more sophisticated analytical tools and methods are required to illuminate the subtleties of classroom interactions and their effects on learning.

The intention of the present book is to elaborate these challenging targets by

- summarising current understandings about the role of classroom interaction in learning;
- presenting a series of original enquiries into aspects of classroom interaction and social learning;
- illustrating some of the implications of these findings in relation to existing insights into classroom interaction and learning;
- introducing an innovative methodological approach to the analysis of collaborative interaction and learning processes in classroom settings.

The book has been structured into three distinct parts. The first part, divided into three chapters, provides an overview of current research on classroom interaction and learning. In addition, it elaborates upon theories of learning and relates them to research on classroom interaction. Chapter 1 gives a short overview of contemporary research investigating classroom interaction and learning. Chapter 2 discusses theoretical perspectives that clarify the meaning of social interaction in learning and instruction. Chapter 3 introduces and describes the emergence of a new analytic framework, which we have been developing in order to investigate collaborative interaction and learning in the classroom.

In the second part of this book we describe a number of case studies investigating the nature of students' classroom interactions across a range of collaborative learning situations. Of particular importance in these studies have been the social conditions and contexts of students' interactions, the emerging patterns and forms of interaction, and their relationship to students' learning. Chapter 4 introduces a study of the nature of students' classroom interaction during whole-class and small-group learning situations, and considers the opportunities that these two classroom organisational systems provide for students' learning. Chapter 5 discusses a study of the nature of students' social interaction in the process of collaborative writing with word processors. This study pays attention to the social learning context created by the use of word processors and how it supports the processes of collaborative writing and learning processes. Chapter 6 draws on a study that focuses on the ways in which leadership and control are constructed and exercised in students' classroom interactions during small-group activities. Chapter 7 discusses a study of collaborative reasoning in student pairs during geometrical problem solving. In this study, particular attention is paid to the social and cognitive dynamics inherent in peer interactions and how they support and challenge productive interaction. Chapter 8 introduces a study of students' collaborative interaction and learning in a multimedia-based setting, during which an electronic encyclopaedia was used as an information resource for the students' poster task. In this study, consideration is directed to the pedagogical conditions for supporting meaningful learning activities with information technology.

The third part of this book draws together the findings of the case studies and relates them to broader theoretical and pedagogical issues of investigating and developing classrooms into interactive learning communities. Chapter 9 summarises key issues emerging from our case studies of students' classroom interactions. In this discussion, we first revisit one of the fundamental findings of this programme of research: a description of the basic functions for which students use language in collaborative learning situations. We then develop this by highlighting the richness of students' classroom interaction in settings embedded in collaborative working modes. We also pay attention to the role of learning tasks and classroom organisation in shaping the nature of students' classroom interactions. The social and cognitive dynamics inherent in students' interactions when working in small groups on open-ended tasks are also considered, in order to highlight features in students' social interaction that mediate their learning processes and outcomes. Our final focus is to consider the role of the teacher as a designer of learning situations as well as a participant in student-centred learning activities.

As authors of this book, we hope that this publication offers the reader new insights into research on classroom interaction and learning. Theoretically, we hope to clarify perspectives on social interaction and learning and to show how they can inform us in creating and monitoring collaborative learning activities in the classroom. The case studies, with their specific research questions and methods, are aimed at providing more information about the processes and conditions for making classrooms into interactive communities. The analytical tools, developed as a part of the case studies for investigating collaborative interactions between students in classroom settings, will hopefully inspire others to use and develop the method towards a new chapter in understanding the practice of learning in social interaction with others.

Part I
Studying classroom interaction and learning

1 Classroom interaction, learning and teaching

Research focusing on the social interactions of the classroom is generally thought to have begun in the 1950s and 60s (see e.g. Bales, 1951; Bellack et al., 1966; Flanders, 1970). During its early phase, educationally oriented research into classroom interaction focused mostly on whole-class interactions between the teacher and students. Among other things, these studies revealed typical classroom interaction patterns, of which the most widely known is the Initiation–Response–Feedback/Evaluation (IRF/E) sequence (Cazden, 1986, 1988; Mehan, 1979; Sinclair and Coulthard, 1975). In this interaction sequence, during which the teacher often tightly controls the structure and content of classroom interaction, the teacher initiates the discussion by posing questions. After the student has responded to the question, the teacher finishes the interaction sequence by giving feedback on the student's response.

Although the identification of typical sequences in classroom settings has increased our understanding of the interactional exchanges between the teacher and students, and highlighted the unequal communicative rights often present in transmission classrooms, it has, nevertheless, been criticised for shedding little light on the communicative functions of interactions and on their consequences for the construction of meaning in the social context of the classroom (Orsolini and Pontecorvo, 1992). Wells (1993) has also shown that, although the exchange structure between the teacher and students may be constant in whole-class discussions, its communicative functions, that is, the purposes for which language is used, may vary widely. Consequently, the triadic interaction sequence may also be identified in teaching episodes conducted according to a view of learning and teaching as a collective meaning-making process.

The gradual change in focus from a transmission model of teaching to learner-sensitive instruction, emphasising collective negotiation in classroom interaction, went hand in hand with the theoretical shift in perspectives on learning and teaching that began to emphasise the active role of individuals in meaning-making and knowledge construction (Wells, 1999). This shift in the theoretical conceptions of learning also began to affect the nature of social interaction in classrooms, transforming classroom interactions from structured discourse patterns to dynamic teaching and learning conversations more typically found in everyday settings. In the latter type of classroom interactions, the role of the student as an active participant in social learning began to be emphasised.

Contemporary views of learning and their pedagogical applications have begun to change traditional classroom interaction patterns, shaping the communicative roles of the teacher and students as participants in a classroom learning community. Post-Vygotskian notions of teaching and learning as assisted performance (Tharp and Gallimore, 1988), or as a process of guided participation (Rogoff, 1990), suggest that learning arises both as the result of deliberate guidance of the learner by a more capable other and, incidentally, through participation in collective activities with the members of the learning community. The central focuses in these metaphors of learning and teaching are on calibrated assistance and the nature of the interactional support that adults or peers can offer to learners.

In following these notions of learning and teaching, Palincsar and Brown (1984) have developed an instructional procedure they call reciprocal teaching, in which students are scaffolded in classroom interaction towards improved reading comprehension. Realised in social interaction between the teacher and students within the context of a small-group activity, reciprocal teaching is supported by four concrete strategies related to text comprehension, namely, questioning, clarifying, summarizing and predicting. In the ongoing interaction, the teacher and the students share the expertise and responsibility of leading the discussion on the contents of the sections of text that they jointly attempt to understand. In the flow of the group discussion, the teacher gives guidance and provides feedback according to the varying needs of the participants. When students are more experienced in participating and leading the discussion, the repetitive structure is gradually given up (Brown and Campione, 1990) and the students can be provided with practice in more complicated argument structures (Brown and Palincsar, 1989). The potential of reciprocal teaching has been widely explored in classroom teaching and learning across various classroom contexts (see e.g. Rosenshine and Meister, 1994). It is also one component of the 'guided discovery in a community of learners' designed by

Brown and Campione (1990) to enhance socially shared expertise in the classroom.

Other researchers, such as Orsolini and Pontecorvo (1992), have also investigated the communicative strategies of the teacher and students in classroom settings, emphasising joint negotiation and meaning-making. In their research, they discovered that in these classrooms the communicative strategies used in whole-class discussions were much wider than during traditional, transmission modes of teaching. For example, the communicative strategies used by the teacher were found to consist of repetition and rephrasing of students' contributions instead of mere questioning and evaluation activity. These strategies seemed to give students more space to participate in classroom discussions and to initiate topics.

Another pedagogical model for classroom interaction and learning, grounded in the sociocultural perspective, is called collective argumentation. This was developed by Brown and Renshaw (2000) in order to create more diverse communicative spaces in the elementary classroom than the conventional interactive practices of teacher-centred classrooms allow. The idea of collective argumentation draws on a number of principles that are required for co-ordinating different perspectives in classroom interaction. These are the principles of generalisability, objectivity and consistency adapted from the work of Miller (1987). In drawing on these principles, a key format of collective argumentation is introduced to the students. The skills of representation, comparison, explanation, justification, agreement and validation are to be used in co-ordinating the phases of their interaction in small groups. The use of these strategies is realized in small group situations in which the teacher first guides the students in sharing their personal views or interpretations of the problem or task in question. This is followed by comparing, explaining and justifying various perspectives in small groups, by establishing a joint agreement, and then by presenting the group's joint representation to the whole class for validation. The teacher's participation in the interactions of the small groups includes allocating management of the problem-solving process to the group, reminding the students about the norms of participation, supporting the development of conjectures and refutations, modelling ways of constructing arguments and the use of appropriate domain-specific language, encouraging the class to engage in the evaluation of co-constructed arguments or perspectives, and providing strategies for dealing with interpersonal conflicts (Brown and Renshaw, 2000).

In their study, Pylvänäinen, Vasama and Kumpulainen (in press) illuminate the modes of teacher participation during whole-class discussions, following the notions of community of inquiry in which value is placed on dialogic and transformative meaning-making between members of the classroom community. In this study, the authors argue for the need to widen the view of the role of the teacher in participating and orchestrating classroom interaction. As their study demonstrates, the teacher's discursive modes in a community of inquiry do not concentrate only on providing cognitive support for the students but also on social and socio-emotional processes. The authors elaborate this argument by identifying four modes of teacher participation in collective inquiry. These are defined as evocative, facilitative, collective and appreciative modes of teacher participation in classroom interaction. In the following, we shall elaborate these modes of participation in some detail, since they also highlight the pedagogical context and its theoretical underpinnings in classroom practice.

In the study of Kovalainen, Kumpulainen and Vasama (in press), the teacher's evocative mode of participation was found to reflect one main principle of the community of inquiry, in which the students were invited and encouraged to ask questions and propose initiations as well as to share and negotiate their opinions and approaches in the classroom community. The evocation of the students' initiations appeared to give the students the opportunity to have local control in choosing the topic for joint inquiry. By evoking the students' views and perspectives, the teacher appeared to make the classroom community co-responsible for their learning, in which there was space for free expression and its communal elaboration. The freedom of choice, including the legitimate control of topics and lines of inquiry, appeared to promote the students' intrinsic motivation for active participation in classroom interaction and learning (Paris and Turner, 1994).

The facilitative mode of participation was found to illuminate the nature of the teacher's scaffolding of the students' reasoning processes in communal inquiry. Among the situated strategies the teacher was observed to use when facilitating classroom interaction were re-voicing questions and interpretations, drawing together perspectives and initiations, modelling and monitoring reasoning processes, and passing on culturally established knowledge and practices. The latter was often highlighted with the active use of cultural metaphors that gave the classroom community tools to approach and conceptualise abstract entities from their own perspectives. The nature of the teacher's facilitation of classroom interaction demonstrates that the interpretative authority of ideas and solutions was distributed in the classroom. Here, all members of the classroom community were responsible for negotiating and evaluating the processes and outcomes of joint problem solving. In fact, it appeared that argumentation and intellectual collaboration were seen as more important than the solution to a problem. The teacher participated as a legitimate member in this process by sensitively calibrating his level of participation from an active listener to that of a guiding tutor. In this study, the teacher did not appear to be an agent whose task was to instil new skills and understanding into the students. Instead, the nature of scaffolding in this classroom was more bi-directional and meanings were socially negotiated, shaped by the students' views and perspectives. Furthermore, in this classroom the reasoning processes and rules that underlay them were made continuously transparent through joint negotiation.

The collective mode of teacher participation reflects the teacher's support of equal participation in joint inquiry as well as tolerance towards different opinions and perspectives. Among the strategies the teacher was found to use for strengthening collectiveness in the classroom were orchestrating turns to speak, promoting collective responsibility and active participation, as well as recalling the rules of participation in the community of inquiry. These means were embedded in the flow of classroom discourse and shaped by the domain-specific topics under investigation. In addition to ensuring the students' equal participation in classroom interaction, the teacher's collective mode of participation appeared to work as an important tool for promoting the students' view of themselves as legitimate members of the learning community.

Another means that seemed to play an important role in community building and scaffolding the students' reasoning processes was the teacher's appreciative mode of participation. The teacher's appreciativeness of the students' initiations, ideas and approaches was reflected in his participation in communal inquiry throughout the study. Another interesting feature relating to the teacher's sensitiveness towards the students was that he paced the tempo of interaction according to the needs of the students. Moreover, in his participation the teacher signalled to the classroom community that he also felt that he could learn from the ongoing discourse. By doing this, the teacher made it explicit that he enjoyed and found reward in being a member of the classroom community.

These analyses of the teacher's participation in classroom interaction also highlighted the nature of the students' roles as learners during a community of inquiry. In this learning community, the students were provided with many opportunities to take initiatives and an active role in initiating and organizing the topics to be investigated. The students also had opportunities to practise various social skills as they jointly worked out problems and co-constructed knowledge in the learning community. In this learning community, the students did not see their teacher as the knowledge-giving authority but instead proudly presented their own ideas and also questioned the assumptions presented by the teacher.

Collaborative interaction in peer groups

Although teacher–student interaction also plays an important role in contemporary classrooms, collaborative working modes with small groups of students have increased in many classrooms as the result of the new conceptions of learning and their pedagogical implications. Consequently, it has become important for teachers and researchers to understand better how meanings and knowledge are constructed between students while working in peer groups on various learning activities. Furthermore, it has become important to understand the kinds of opportunities provided for learning in such classrooms, and the possible obstacles that may hinder effective problem solving and learning in peer groups. In addition to understanding the dynamics and nature of the social and cognitive processes that underlie interactions in collaborative peer groups, it is also important to understand what kind of instructional support students need in these activity settings.

Social interaction among student groups tends to differ from traditional teacher–student interaction in its degree of reciprocity (Forman, 1989). In teacher–student interactions, it is often the teacher who controls the content of interaction and the distribution of speaking turns. In peer interaction, turn taking and selection of content is distributed among the students (Rommetveit, 1985). Students who have the responsibility for managing their own talk must cope with silences, negotiate how, when and who talks, and assess the relevance and quality of communication (Barnes and Todd, 1977, 1995). Consequently, classroom interaction among students, in which different opinions, definitions and interpretations are expressed and created, is usually complex and dynamic in nature (Cohen, 1994; Hicks, 1995; Maybin, 1991). Moreover, in peer interaction, the communicative options available to students, during which each may take turns at instructing the other, are much wider (Forman, 1989). These extended opportunities for using language and participating in classroom interactions seem to give students ample opportunities for joint meaning-making and knowledge construction. Yet, the dynamic and free-flowing nature of interaction in peer groups also poses new challenges and responsibilities for students engaging in productive classroom communication and learning.

Working in collaborative peer groups is reported to help the students to construct and become aware of their own thinking processes. When sharing their views and perspectives with others, the students can discover divergent ways of approaching phenomena and solving problems. Moreover, they can build on each other's contributions to re-construct new interpretations and views that were yet to be discovered. The practice of sharing and constructing perspectives in collaborative interaction is also assumed to promote reflection, planning and metacognition (Arvaja *et al.*, 2000).

Although we are still remarkably ignorant about the dynamics and processes of peer group interaction and learning, studies of co-operative learning and peer tutoring in different instructional settings have identified specific interactions that seem to promote learning. These forms of interaction have included providing explanations (Webb, Troper and Fall, 1995), asking appropriate questions (King, 1989) and exchanging ideas, explanations, justifications, speculations, inferences, hypotheses and conclusions (Cohen, 1994). Of importance also seems to be the provision of sufficient time for participants to think before responding (Graesser and Person, 1994) and the use of supportive communication skills such as giving feedback and encouragement (Webb and Farivar, 1994).

Some research studies, inspired by sociocultural perspectives on learning, have also tried to identify different interaction patterns and episodes that can be conducive to learning both in whole-class and small-group activities. Mercer (1994), Phillips (1990) and Fisher (1993), for example, have shown how exploratory and argumentative talk can be more effective in fostering students' critical thinking than procedural or routinised interactions. As they put it, exploratory talk includes a constructive and critical engagement with ideas and meanings generated in the ongoing discussion and is characterised by statements with justifications and alternative hypotheses. For them, knowledge is made publicly accountable and reasoning is visible in exploratory discussions.

Despite promising findings in relation to the power of collaborative peer group interaction to support learning, the portrait of collaborative interaction emerging from research seems to be less positive (Hogan, Nastasi and Pressley, 2000). Micro-level analyses of the interaction processes inherent in student groups have shown that instead of engaging in joint reasoning problem solving, the students tend to concentrate on completing a task. In these learning situations, peer interaction is likely to be product oriented, in which individual problem solving may play a bigger role than that of collaborative meaning-making (Kumpulainen and Mutanen, 1998). Furthermore, cognitive conflicts may result in social conflicts, leading easily to dominance or breakdown of the collaborative learning activity. The social status of the students in the classroom may also affect the level of student participation and engagement in collaborative working and learning.

The students' communication skills and habits also play a role in mediating productive collaborative interaction (Bennett and Dunne, 1991). Students do not always engage in giving arguments, making hypotheses, providing explanations and elaborating or justifying their actions or views through their verbal interaction. The students may use imprecise language when communicating their views to their peers. All these elements challenge the reciprocity between interactors that is, apparently, necessary for collaborative meaning-making.

Although there is evidence that collaborative interaction in peer groups can promote learning, there are still many barriers to its success. These barriers can include, among other things, interpersonal dynamics and the nature of the learning situations in which collaborative interaction takes place. In the second part of this book we describe a number of case studies that focus on elaborating these issues in more detail. They also highlight the necessity to investigate collaborative peer interaction with dynamic and multi-level analysis tools.

To summarise, recent studies of classroom interaction provide evidence of the existence of varied and, in many ways, new patterns and forms of interaction in contemporary classrooms. Although these classroom interactions are closer to everyday conversations, it should not be forgotten that there is a difference between everyday and school-based interactions. This difference lies in the fact that classrooms are – or at least should be – intentionally oriented towards learning. This is not necessarily the case in everyday conversations in out-of-school contexts, although learning can and often does take place in such contexts as well. The reason for emphasising this is that it is the educational value of social interactions, including the mechanisms and patterns that lead to intended learning goals, that are the prime concern for interaction studies within the discipline of education.

2 Perspectives on social interaction and learning

The role of social interaction in learning and instruction has attracted many researchers from different disciplines and has been studied from, at least, linguistic, sociological and anthropological perspectives (see e.g. Edwards and Westgate, 1987, 1994). Research into classroom interaction has, therefore, been underpinned by a number of different theoretical perspectives on learning and development, each with its own theoretical analysis of the role of such interaction in learning. Despite the cross-disciplinary significance of these learning theories in increasing our understanding of the role of social interaction in learning and instruction, they cannot by any means be regarded as consistent with each other. The distinction made in the discussion below between the sociocultural and cognitive views of learning attempts to demonstrate some of these inconsistencies. These inconsistencies are interesting in many ways since, in addition to theoretical orientation, they are reflected in research designs and methodologies, which have obvious consequences for the understanding of the relationship between interaction and learning.

In this chapter we will examine two of the dominant theoretical perspectives on learning: the sociocultural and cognitive perspectives. These perspectives should be seen as umbrella terms that have each stimulated research studies with apparently similar aims but with marked differences in terms of the theoretical and methodological positions from which they approach their enquiries.

The sociocultural perspective

Sociocultural views of learning rest on theories that emphasise the social nature of development. The most influential of these theories is based on the work of L. S. Vygotsky and his followers (see e.g. Davydov, 1995; Leontjev, 1981; Vygotsky 1962, 1978; Wertsch,

1991). The sociocultural perspective has also been influenced by socio-logical theories about the social construction of reality (e.g. Berger and Luckmann, 1966; Mead, 1934) and by anthropological studies on the relationship between learning and culture (e.g. Spindler and Spindler 1955).

The sociocultural perspective emphasises the situatedness of think-ing and speaking in the context of activity (Wertsch, Hagström and Kikas, 1995). According to this perspective, an individual's mental activity can be understood only by investigating it within its cultural, historical and institutional context. Central to the sociocultural perspective is the fact that any mental activity should be investigated as an interaction between social agents and physical environment. The perspective emphasises the social and situated nature of knowledge formation, with cognition being seen as including action distributed and constructed with others in cultural contexts, including the use of tools and symbols formed by the culture. Social situations are, hence, seen as creating knowledge through action with more knowledgeable members of the community. Knowledge is viewed not as a self-sufficient substance detachable from situations in which it is created but rather as something inseparable from those activities in which it is constructed and applied (Brown, Collins and Duguid, 1989).

Researchers working from a sociocultural perspective study the learner as part of his/her social context and, hence, social interaction and context are not separated from the learning situation. The role of culturally developed sign systems, such as language, are stressed in social interaction since they are regarded as tools for thinking and the construction of socially shared meanings. The individual learns to understand world and self through semiotic tools, which are seen as having personal, social and cultural importance. Central to the socio-cultural perspective on learning is the concept of internalisation, which defines learning as proceeding from the social, intermental plane to the individual's intramental plane of understanding. The movement from social to individual is regarded as a complex and transformative process that is supported by active participation and assistance pro-vided by other members of the learning community (Vygotsky, 1978).

The pedagogical applications of the sociocultural perspective have included the development of innovative instructional settings and pedagogical practices. In these pedagogical developments, emphasis is often placed on providing learners with the opportunity to engage in their zones of proximal development supported by social interaction with more knowledgeable members of the culture. Among the peda-gogical developments could be mentioned concepts such as *scaffolding and contingent instruction* (Wood, Bruner and Ross, 1976), *cognitive apprenticeship* (Rogoff, 1990), *legitimate peripheral participation* (Lave and Wenger, 1991) and *the negotiation of meaning in the construction zone* (Newman, Griffin and Cole, 1989). All these developments stress the learner's active participation in social interaction and emphasise the conceptualisation of learning as a process of enculturation in which the learner gradually becomes a more active participant in cultural activities. In addition, they stress goal-oriented learning activity in situations that are authentic and meaningful in relation to the application of knowledge to be learned. From the point of view of social interaction, these pedagogical developments emphasise intersubjectivity between the interactors and the importance of common understanding and shared history for its establishment.

The cognitive perspective

The cognitive perspective on learning consists of a number of theories that differ in the emphasis they give to the relationship between an individual and social context. At one end of the continuum is the radical view, which emphasises the individual's mental processes in the construction of knowledge (von Glasersfeld, 1989). At the other end is the socio-cognitive or socio-constructivist view, which pays more attention to the social context in which the individual is acting and in which knowledge is constructed. Depending on emphasis, the concept of social context is regarded as the immediate context in which activity occurs, although sometimes attention is also paid to the wider socio-cultural context of that activity (Resnick, 1989). In the following discussion, the cognitive perspective refers to Piaget's developmental theory and to cognitive psychology in general.

The cognitive perspective on learning emphasises the individual's mental activity, the development of thinking, cognitive strategies and their application. In the light of this perspective, learning is seen as a process during which the individual organises his/her activity in order to eliminate conflicts and imbalance (disequilibrium) (von Glasersfeld, 1989). Special attention is given to the individual's goals and purposes, which lay grounds for learning. Special stress is also laid upon developmental processes, since development is seen as making possible the conditions for learning (Piaget, 1954).

The cognitive perspective focuses on individuals and their learning. At the beginning of an individual's development, he/she is seen as an egocentric who gradually develops into a social being. The cognitive perspective regards interaction as supporting the individual's knowledge construction, since it helps to activate existing knowledge in the individual. Social interaction is seen as helping the individual to understand and become aware of thinking processes, since the explication and organisation of thought in speech assists the reorganisation of knowledge. On the other hand, while listening to others the learner is able to compare different interpretations and points of view. The disagreements confronted during the interaction may cause cognitive conflicts, which, after being solved, stimulate cognitive reorganisation, or accommodation in Piaget's terms, in the individual (Doise and Mugny, 1984).

The cognitive perspective emphasises psychologically equal interaction, in which individuals co-ordinate their actions towards a common goal while acknowledging the perspectives and orientation of other participating individuals. Reciprocity between individuals creates a psychological base for perspective taking and assists the individual to see things from different angles. Psychologically equal interaction between individuals is seen as enabling the creation of conflict situations relevant for the construction of knowledge (DeVries, 1997).

Although the cognitive perspective on learning has traditionally focused its attention on the individual's learning processes, such as the development of mental structures, knowledge handling and meta-cognitive skills, and has seen social interaction as only one factor affecting learning, recently more attention has begun to be paid to the social context in which learning occurs. In this sense, the cognitive perspective has come closer to the sociocultural view of learning. However, there are still distinct differences between the perspectives.

Contrasting the perspectives

The sociocultural and cognitive perspectives both emphasise the role of *action* in learning. The sociocultural view stresses participation in cultural activities, whereas the cognitive perspective gives priority to the individual's sensorimotor and conceptual activity. The sociocultural view assumes that cognitive processes are part of social and cultural processes. The social dimension of consciousness is thus given priority over the individual dimension, since individual consciousness is seen as being constructed through social activity in the zone of proximal development (Vygotsky, 1978). Whilst the advocates of a cognitive perspective analyse cognition and thinking as conceptual processes that are located in the individual, socioculturalists, on the other hand, take social action as the unit of analysis (cf. Cobb,

1994). Crucial to the latter view are the means whereby participation in interaction and in other culturally organised activities is associated with the individual's development.

The second difference between the perspectives is found in the definition of *thinking*. In other words, is thinking located in the individual or in social activity? Whilst the cognitive perspective conceptualises thinking as an activity in the individual's mind, the sociocultural perspective does not separate thinking from its social context but rather examines it as social action.

The third topic of controversy is the concept of *development*. Should development be viewed as a process of cognitive reorganisation or as a process of enculturation into culturally specified practices (cf. Cobb, 1994)? The cognitive perspective approaches development from the cognitive organisational point of view, whereas in a sociocultural perspective the emphasis is upon enculturation.

The role of *signs and symbols* in learning is viewed differently from each of the two perspectives. Whilst the cognitive perspective has a tendency to acknowledge their significance in terms of tools to express and communicate thinking, researchers guided by a sociocultural perspective examine the social histories of signs and symbols. This difference is also reflected in the distinct roles accorded to oral language in relation to the individual and social group. From the cognitive perspective, speech reflects an individual's thinking, providing visible evidence, for example, of the cognitive strategies employed. A sociocultural approach, on the other hand, emphasises the social conditions of interaction and the historical context of social activity (Wertsch, 1991). Discourse and speech are seen as jointly created and reflecting the meaning-making process between the participants. The sociocultural perspective emphasises the dialogic and multi-voicedness nature of language (Bakhtin, 1986). According to this view, an utterance does not only belong to the individual but is shaped by its sociohistorical and immediate social context.

Although the cognitive and sociocultural perspectives differ from one another in many essential respects, they do have similarities in their conceptions of the dynamic nature of knowledge construction. According to both perspectives, knowledge is not a static, given commodity, but is, rather, shaped and created as the result of a constructive activity. From a cognitive perspective, these are inner construction processes, whereas from the sociocultural perspective, reciprocal negotiation and meaning-making in a social context are much more significant.

Social interaction and learning – separate or joint concepts?

Although the cognitive view has not traditionally examined learning or the development of an individual from a social perspective, it would be wrong to claim that the cognitive view has failed completely to acknowledge the social element in learning and development (cf. DeVries, 1997). The major difference between the cognitive and socio-cultural perspectives lies not in whether they acknowledge the significance of interaction and social context in learning, but in the definition of the relationship between interaction and learning. In other words, is learning social and situated by its nature or do social and contextual features affect learning? Is interaction an aspect of learning or is it something logically independent that has a function in learning? Can learning be explained by the nature of interaction?

The cognitive perspective often sees interaction as a factor that affects learning. Learning is seen as a variable that can be partly explained by the characteristics of interaction and social context (Doise and Mugny, 1984). In the sociocultural perspective, however, interaction and context are not separated from one another. The individual and his/her environment (physical and social) are viewed in a dialectical relationship. Consequently, the individual's action is seen as part of the social construction of shared understanding (inter-subjectivity) (Wertsch, 1991).

The conceptual differences between these theoretical perspectives are also reflected in empirical studies of interaction and learning in educational contexts. In the next section, we discuss these differences by highlighting some empirical and methodological characteristics of interaction studies located either on the cognitive or sociocultural continuum of learning theories.

Studies of social interaction in learning

In the following, some empirical and methodological features of educationally oriented interaction studies will be examined. A distinction is made between studies applying cognitive or sociocultural perspectives to social interaction and learning. The main goal is to highlight different ways of analysing social interaction in learning and also to lay the foundation for the development of a dynamic approach to the analysis of classroom interaction.

The individual and the group

Interaction studies following the cognitive perspective have traditionally directed their attention to the individual's activity in social contexts, during which the effects of interaction on the individual's learning, for example on the development of conceptual structures, have been studied. Experimental research studies have often investigated the individual's performance on a cognitive task before and after a social interaction situation (e.g. Forman, 1989). In addition, investigations have studied the effectiveness of small-group work in relation to individual work and tried to identify effective forms of interaction in relation to learning (e.g. Light *et al.*, 1994). There are also sociocognitive studies that have paid more attention to the qualitative differences in the individual's goals and situational definitions of the learning task and investigated how these are associated with the individual's participation in social activity (e.g. Grossen, 1994).

Interaction studies following the sociocultural perspective have usually concentrated on describing the activities of a social group, characterising its features, forms and nature. The primary goal has often been to understand the process of enculturation and internalisation. For these studies it has become important to investigate how individuals participate in educational activities and how they jointly construct their social thinking in cultural contexts (e.g. Berqvist and Säljö, 1995; Mercer, 2000). The social activity observed is regarded as reflecting the practices, traditions and values of the social group under investigation. In the sociocultural perspective, minor attention is paid to the role of the individual as a constructor, interpreter and appropriator of joint knowledge.

Contextuality and generality

The level of acknowledgement given to the contextual nature of social interaction varies according to the theoretical orientation of interaction studies. Studies aimed at producing comparisons between various social settings have often used pre-defined categories of interaction in their analyses, whereas studies emphasising the situated character of interaction have used more interpretative and qualitative methods. Both methods have their strengths and their problems. Clearly defined categories of interaction provide comparable data about interaction in different settings, but, at the same time, understanding the contextual nature of the social activities they study is made more difficult, since the data is often quantified and detached from the social context into neatly defined 'packages'. On the other hand, the challenges for context-specific analyses of interaction concern the generalisability and comparability of the research results (Edwards and Westgate, 1994). Interaction studies applying the cognitive perspective on social interaction and learning have used both quantitative and, particularly recently, qualitative analysis methods, aiming at contextual and meaning level analyses. In general, however, such studies have analysed interactional phenomena using clearly pre-defined categories. In the analysis of interaction, concentration has been given, for example, to problem-solving strategies, such as questions, summaries, explaining and predicting. The relationship of these to learning and their effectiveness as learning tools have also been investigated (e.g. King, 1989, 1992; Nastasi and Clements, 1992).

Socioculturally oriented interaction research already sees interaction as part of the context and, consequently, does not differentiate the situation from analysis of it. From this perspective, every utterance is a 'microcosm' of the whole social context, including participants' situational definitions, orientation and the sociohistorical framework of the activity (Wertsch, 1991). On the basis of this theoretical approach, studies often concentrate on the analysis of larger sociohistorical phenomena in which activity is embedded (e.g. Rogoff and Toma, 1997) and also on micro-level analysis, since they are seen as closely connected to macro-level phenomena (e.g. Hogan, Nastasi and Pressley, 2000; Hoogsteder, Meier and Elbers, 1996). These studies have used both qualitative and quantitative analyses, but crucial to them is always a knowledge of the sociohistorical and cultural framework of an activity.

Static description and dynamic description

The description and analysis of interaction in a static manner is more typical of interaction research following the cognitive perspective on learning. In practice, this means that episodes, turns or even shorter expressions, such as utterances, are detached from the interaction as a whole on the basis of theoretical presumptions. The analysis of interaction can be carried out using pre-defined categories, or more or less defined categorisations are created as the result of a retrospective analysis of the interaction. The result of such analysis is often a rather static and fragmented picture of the interactional phenomena, which can be presented numerically, by counting the frequency of analytical categories, or qualitatively, by describing categories with extracts. As an example, one could mention studies conducted by

Webb and her co-researchers, who have extensively researched pupil–pupil interaction in small-group work situations. In these studies, helping behaviour, for example, is detached from the interaction data and its relationship to students' learning is investigated (e.g. Webb, Troper and Fall, 1995).

In research stemming from the sociocultural perspective, it is usual to describe interaction as action in process. To emphasise this view, a number of researchers have begun to talk about the dynamic nature of interaction (see e.g. Kumpulainen and Mutanen, 1999). Although the analysis of the dynamic nature of interaction is still a methodological challenge, the application of conversational analysis and discourse analysis has offered some tools to understand the evolving nature of social interaction. Conversation analysis aims at understanding how participants organise their speaking turns and topics in an interaction situation. It concentrates on describing the sequential development of conversation, i.e. the logical–chronological structures of interaction, aiming to highlight the construction of turns in conversation. Discourse analysis aims to highlight the process of communication, interaction, understandings and their maintenance. Discourse analysis is often linked to the work of Sinclair and Coulthard (1975), who characterised teacher-directed discourse in classrooms. Their analysis is multi-layered and it concentrates on speech acts, moves, exchanges and transactions.

These methods do not 'freeze' interaction into pieces but, rather, characterise the construction of interaction and its meanings on an utterance-by-utterance or turn-by-turn basis. The application of conversation analysis and discourse analysis alongside meaning-level analysis has begun to provide information about meaning construction processes in interaction as well as to highlight participants' roles and identities in interaction situations (Elbers and Streefland, 2000). The emphasis on the dynamic and process-oriented character of interaction in the sociocultural perspective is explained by its stress on the dynamics of meaning construction. According to this perspective, meanings develop not in one utterance but rather in chains of utterances and in longer episodes. These chains of meanings are not easily identifiable, since they carry multiple meanings within them (Bakhtin, 1986).

Meanings of discourse and forms of discourse

In analysing social interaction, it is necessary to refer to a *content dimension*, i.e. the nature of the meanings carried by the interaction, and an *interactional dimension*, i.e. the form and structure taken by those meanings (Brown and Yule, 1983). Interaction studies underpinned by a cognitive view of learning typically concentrate on the forms and functions of discourse and interaction, whereas socioculturally based studies tend to investigate the construction of meaning in interaction. This analytical difference derives from the fact that the cognitive perspective considers language to reflect more or less the individual's thinking and learning strategies, whereas the sociocultural perspective stresses intersubjectivity and the construction of meanings in interaction. Central to the sociocultural view, consequently, are the meanings of interaction, i.e. content, as well as the forms and structures in which they are created, such as the coherence of interaction.

Summary

Interaction studies basing their theoretical background on the cognitive perspective take the individual's activity as their unit of analysis and see interaction as reflecting his/her thinking processes. Studies derived from the sociocultural perspective tend, on the other hand, to investigate the activities of a social group, for example by focusing on their participation structure, and to view interaction as a social construction. From the cognitive perspective, interaction analysis often takes place through theoretically derived categories that fragment interaction as static, whereas a characteristic of a sociocultural approach is its attempt to understand the social context in which interaction takes place as well as the dynamic and process-oriented nature of interaction and meaning-making. Emphasis is given not only to the meanings of interaction and discourse but also to its structures. These distinctions are summarised in table 1.

When investigating theoretical and methodological differences between studies of social interaction and learning, it is important to point out that they are not always reflected as distinctively and clearly in individual studies as the generalisations made above might suggest. In recent years particularly, a theoretical and methodological integration has begun to develop, and it is increasingly common for studies to attempt, more or less consciously, to integrate theoretical conceptions of learning and methodological orientations.

Interaction research: strengths and problems

Our examination of theoretical perspectives and their reflection in studies of social interaction and learning has shown that socioculturally

Table 1 Theoretical orientation and characteristics of styles of interaction research

	Constructivist perspective	Sociocultural perspective
Focus of analysis	Individual	Group
Definition for speech and discourse	Reflection of the individual's thinking	A social construction through which meanings are co-created
Typical features of interaction analysis	• Acknowledge the immediate context of interaction (micro-level analyses)	• Acknowledge the sociocultural context of interaction (macro- and micro-level analyses)
	• Quantitative analyses aiming at comparable information, pre-defined categories of interaction	• Qualitative analyses, meaning level analyses
	• Static description of interaction	• Dynamic description of interaction
	• Focus on the functions and forms of interaction	• Focus on the meanings and structures of interaction

oriented interaction studies often locate social interaction in a larger activity system, for example by taking account of the school as a social institution. Central research topics for this line of investigation are the meaning-making processes in interaction, cultural practices, forms of participation, rules, values and identities, and through these the characterisation of culturally and situationally defined prerequisites for learning.

Cognitively oriented interaction studies are interested in the development of knowing in the individual via social interaction. In addition, they concentrate on investigating interaction as a reflection of, and an influence upon, the individual's thinking. Central to the cognitive perspective is the investigation of the individual's knowledge structures, cognitive strategies and situational definitions and their connection to the knowledge construction process.

Whereas the sociocultural perspective sees classroom interactions as culturally patterned activities that are constructed and appropriated, the cognitive perspective views classroom interaction as a developing micro-culture that is associated with the teacher's and students' attempts to co-ordinate their own and each other's activities. The sociocultural perspective emphasises the homogeneity of a cultural group and does not lay stress on individual differences in thinking. The cognitive perspective, on the other hand, emphasises individuality and avoids generalising cultural and social practices (cf. Cobb, 1994).

The strengths of the sociocultural perspective on learning can be seen in the fact that it has widened knowledge of the concept of learning by emphasising its cultural and situational embeddedness. Its weaknesses, however, are perhaps found in its inability to provide concrete information about the individual's learning processes or how to organise effective learning situations (Anderson, Reder and Simon, 1997). The emphasis on the sociocultural situatedness of learning has also given some problems in interaction analysis in terms of defining the focus of research: from how wide a perspective should one investigate the phenomena of interaction?

The cognitive view has, on the other hand, increased understanding of the development of the individual's knowledge structures and the organisation of learning situations. Its weakness has been that it has not paid enough attention to the social context in which learning and interaction takes place. In other words, whereas the constructivist perspective has been able to provide information about the content of learning, it has been unsuccessful in characterising the features of learning situations that are linked to the construction of knowledge (Vosniadou, 1996).

Theoretical integration and the challenges of interaction research

The integration of the theoretical conceptions of the sociocultural and cognitive perspectives has begun to be noticeable in recent studies of social interaction and learning (e.g. Salomon, 1997). Learning seems to be becoming viewed as a process of self-organisation and enculturation into a culture. Greater emphasis tends to be given to social and contextual features of the learning process (Anderson, Reder and Simon, 1997; Greeno, 1997). An increasingly important task for educational research is to try to understand the complex relationship between an individual's mental activities and interpretations as well as to recognise the socio-cultural embeddedness of learning and teaching

(Vosniadou, 1996). Conceptions of mind have begun to change from that of an information-processing machine to that of a developing biological system that acts and develops in a complex physical, social and cultural environment. The role of the mind as both an interpreter and a constructor of culture is also recognised. Thinking is seen as being located both in the individual as well as in the tools and symbol systems created by culture (Salomon, 1993).

In the midst of these changes in the views of learning, educationally and psychologically oriented interaction research has confronted new theoretical and methodological challenges. The first challenge, which is more theoretical in nature, concerns the changing conceptions of the relationship between interaction and learning. In the light of recent theoretical integration, it seems that interaction and learning cannot be thought of as causally linked but rather should be seen as part of the social context in which learning occurs. Consequently, the relationship between learning and interaction must be viewed as extremely complex. Learning and interaction processes that evolve in instructional settings should be seen as constructed by the participants, shaped by their intentions and interpretations. From this perspective, interaction research focusing on learning and teaching processes should be understood as an interpretative construction of interactional phenomena whose aim is to describe, interpret and predict the social activities and learning processes constructed by the participants in a goal-oriented pedagogical activity (Kumpulainen and Mutanen, 1999).

Another challenge for interaction research is a methodological one and it concerns the data collection procedures and analytical approaches to be used. It appears that methodological tools need to take a more dynamic approach to social interaction. This means that the study of interaction needs to use a range of methods and time scales. Interaction analyses need to approach interaction from the individual's perspective, by taking account of personal perceptions of the situations in which the individual is engaged, individual goals and previous experience, as well as from the social perspective, by acknowledging the ecology of particular forms of interaction and the sociohistorical background to learning situations. This includes acknowledging both the meanings and forms of interaction. In addition, analyses need to pay attention to the immediate and sociohistorical context of the activity in which the learner is located. The dynamics of these features need to be examined using methods that are context sensitive but that give the possibility of comparisons across studies. Interaction analysis should not only concentrate on verbal interaction but needs to acknowledge the role of other psychological and physical tools as constructors of meaning. On the whole, there is a need for multi-layered analysis models whose layers support one another and facilitate cross-examination. Possible areas for cross-examination are, for example, linguistic, psychological and cultural analyses of interaction (Mercer, 1996). In addition to the development of analytical tools for interaction analysis, new models of data presentation are needed. Instead of the oversimplifications characteristic of much interaction research data, there is a need for new means of relevantly justifying the use of extracts as examples characterising the reality investigated.

3 An introduction to a method of analysis of classroom interaction

The social and contextual nature of human learning has received great emphasis in recent research on learning and instruction (Anderson, Reder and Simon, 1997; Greeno, 1997), and more attention has been paid to the practices, processes and conditions leading to the social construction of knowledge in different learning situations (Fisher, 1993; Lemke, 1990; Palincsar, 1986; Tuyay, Jennings and Dixon, 1995). The focus of analysis has been extended from external factors influencing learning processes and achievements to the student's participation in and evolving interpretations of the learning activity (Grossen, 1994; Perret-Clermont, Perret and Bell, 1991). In the midst of these changes in emphasis, new methodological questions concerning the analysis of classroom interaction and learning have arisen. Questions to which researchers have been trying to find answers are, for example:

- How can we show qualitative differences within and between interactive activities across learning contexts and arrangements?
- Upon what criteria should such judgements be made?
- How applicable are the methods used?

(Westgate and Hughes, 1997)

In this chapter we will introduce a descriptive system of analysis for investigating the dynamics of peer interactive groups. The analysis framework has emerged as a result of a number of studies we have conducted of primary-aged students' interactions while working in peer groups on various educational tasks (Fourlas and Wray, 1990; Kumpulainen, 1994, 1996; Kumpulainen and Mutanen, 1998, 1999). The main goal in these studies has been to investigate the nature of students' social activity, particularly verbal interaction, in different small-group work-learning situations. The initial development of the method concentrated on the functions of students' verbal interaction as a basis for investigation of students' roles as communicators and learners in teacher-centred and peer group-centred classrooms (Fourlas and Wray, 1990). This functional analysis method was later piloted, modified and applied by Kumpulainen (1994, 1996) in a study that investigated students' social interaction during the process of collaborative writing with a word processor. Due to its fine-grained categorisations, the functional analysis method was felt to give a structured overview of the nature and quality of students' verbal interaction in this learning context.

Despite the potential of the analysis method, in our recent studies of peer group learning we have found this functional analysis of verbal interaction to be inadequate as a means of unravelling the complexities of socially shared learning processes. Firstly, there seemed to be a need to develop a descriptive system of analysis that took a more holistic and multi-dimensional perspective on interaction. Consequently, the analysis of verbal interaction alone seemed not to be sufficient for this. Secondly, it seemed important that more attention be paid to the moment-by-moment nature of interaction in order to highlight the situated processes of meaning-making and knowledge construction within peer groups. Thirdly, it seemed important to take the individual and the group as units of analysis in order to investigate the types and forms of participation within peer groups. In addition to methodological developments, there seemed to be a need to develop more efficient models of interaction data presentation.

In the analysis method we have currently been developing, the dynamics of peer group interaction are approached from three analytic dimensions.

- The first dimension of the analysis, termed the *functional analysis*, investigates the character and purpose of student utterances in peer group interaction. It characterises the communicative strategies used by participants in social interaction.
- The second dimension, *cognitive processing*, examines the ways in which students approach and process learning tasks in their social interaction. It aims to highlight students' working strategies and situated positions towards learning, knowledge and themselves as problem-solvers.
- The third dimension of the analysis, *social processing*, focuses on the nature of the social relationships that are developed during students' social activity. This includes examining the types and forms of student participation in social interaction.

Before discussing the theoretical and methodological background of our methods and highlighting the analytical framework with some empirical examples, we shall first review some of the other analysis methods used to study peer interaction that have contributed to the present analytical approach.

Investigating collaborative interaction in peer groups

Peer group interaction has already been studied quite extensively in different contexts in and out of school. The research objectives and methodological solutions have been diverse, being linked with the research goals and theoretical perspectives adopted by the researchers. One large group of studies focusing on peer interaction from the educational perspective is located in the systematic tradition, often referred to as process–product studies of peer interaction (e.g. Joiner *et al.*, 1995; King, 1989; Light *et al.*, 1994; Teasley, 1995; Tudge, 1992; Webb, Troper and Fall, 1995). In these studies, peer interaction is analysed with coding schemes that categorise interaction into pre-defined categories. Variables such as student achievement and performance are statistically linked to the frequency of categories as identified in the data. Usually, the development of the actual interaction process or meaning-making in interaction is not the prime interest, but the focus is rather on some specific features of the interaction and their relationship to student learning or achievement. Consequently, the process of interaction over a period of time is not highlighted by such studies. The situated nature of interaction, as represented by the contextual features impinging upon it, also often receives only cursory inspection. One advantage of process–product studies is that they enable the analysis of large amounts of data and use publicly verifiable criteria to make their categorisations.

Perhaps the best-known early researchers of peer group talk and learning are Barnes and Todd (1977, 1995), who developed an analytic system for studying peer group talk. Their system of analysis was 'grounded' in the data, as opposed to being derived from a pre-existing network of categories. Consequently, their system does try to take account of the context in which peer talk occurs. In their analysis, Barnes and Todd were interested in the actual processes of interaction. They were interested in the ways in which students developed and constructed knowledge without direct teacher presence. They make a distinction between the interactive and the social aspects of speech events. This was achieved by the use of a two-level parallel analysis that, at the first level, focused on the coherence of the discourse and, at the second level, concentrated on the social skills and cognitive strategies employed by the students in their discourse. While conducting their study on peer group talk across a range of discussion tasks, Barnes and Todd realised how difficult it was to identify logical relationships from peer interaction, since these are more often left implicit than given a verbal form. The fact that Barnes and Todd had only tape recordings of peer talk made the analysis even more difficult in terms of logical development. Despite some limitations found in the analytical system and the tools used for data collection, Barnes and Todd's work made an important contribution to the analysis of peer talk, since it integrated ideas from discourse and conversational analysis with research on learning and instruction, and their definitions of *content frames* and *interaction frames* made it possible to investigate how students brought their frames of reference to the interaction situation and how these frames were jointly negotiated and developed.

Many other methods of analysis of peer group interaction, either with distinct categories or more interpretative 'modes', have been developed in the past twenty years, and to review all of them here would be impossible. One recent analytic approach that has contributed to our understanding of children's talk during small-group learning is that developed by Fisher (1993), Mercer (1994, 1996) and Phillips (1990), the researchers involved in the SLANT (Spoken Language And New Technologies) project (see Mercer, Phillips and Somekh, 1991). What is interesting in this approach is that it tries to investigate how children use talk to think together, thus it uses a group as a unit of analysis, not individual children. By taking a sociocultural approach to children's talk, it tries to show that particular ways of talking permit certain social modes of thinking. The analytic framework was derived from analyses of children's talk during collaborative peer group learning with computers and it includes three distinct modes of talk that characterise different ways of thinking together. These are:

- disputational mode, characterised by disagreement and individualised decision making;
- cumulative mode, consisting of positive but uncritical decision making;
- exploratory mode, which is seen as the most effective mode of speaking in fostering critical thinking and cognitive development (Mercer, 1996). This is characterised by constructive and critical engagements, including argumentation and hypothesis testing.

Theoretically, this analytical framework makes an important contribution to our increasing understanding of the different modes of talk and social thinking in peer group situations. One of the limitations of the method, though, can be found in the fact that the unit of analysis is the group – the method does not take into account individual students' participation in the 'social modes of thinking'. Consequently, the method does not highlight how the different types of social thinking are actually constructed within peer groups. Moreover, by concentrating mainly on students' talk, the analysis may not always give a complete picture of the nature of knowledge construction in peer groups. Instead, a more dynamic approach to peer interaction that focuses on the whole interactive context and its development, including non-verbal communication and the use of different tools, is necessary before we can unravel the processes and conditions for learning in peer group activity.

Towards a new analytic method

In this chapter we will outline and discuss a descriptive system of analysis for investigating the situated dynamics of peer group interaction. Of particular importance are the mechanisms through which the social and cognitive features of peer group activity operate. In addition, the forms, patterns and relationships between peer group interaction, problem solving and learning are considered. The theoretical grounding of the analysis framework is informed by the sociocultural and sociocognitive perspectives to interaction and learning (Cole, 1996; Resnick, Levine and Teasley, 1991; Wertsch, 1985, 1991), whereas the methodological solutions presented are greatly influenced by the work of Barnes and Todd (1977, 1995) and Mercer (1994, 1996) as well as by interactional ethnographers (Green and Mayer, 1991; Green and Wallat, 1981; Tuyay, Jennings and Dixon, 1995).

In our method, learning is seen to take place as a result of individuals' active participation in the practices of the social environment. Learning is viewed as an interactional process that requires an understanding of language and other semiotic tools as both personal and social resources (Cole, 1996; Halliday and Hasan, 1989; Wells and Chang-Wells, 1992). Peer interaction is treated as a dynamic process in which language and other semiotic tools are used as instruments of communication and learning. Interaction is seen as a complex social phenomenon composed of non-verbal and social properties in addition to its verbal characteristics. Peer discourse itself is treated not as representing a person's inner cognitive world, or even as descriptive of an outer reality, but rather as a tool-in-action shaped by participants' culturally based definitions of the situation (Edwards, 1993; Edwards and Potter, 1992).

The application of the method involves a micro-analysis of evolving peer interactions by focusing on three analytic dimensions, namely the functions of verbal interaction, cognitive processing and social processing. Whereas the functional analysis concentrates on students' verbal language, the analyses of students' cognitive and social processing focus on interactive dynamics as they occur across the participants. Consequently, a group is taken as a unit of analysis. The three dimensions are treated separately for analytic purposes, although it is recognised that they are closely linked together in a complex way. In actuality, the dimensions cannot be separated, since each element gives meaning to all others and simultaneously obtains meaning from them.

Dimension 1: Functional analysis of verbal interaction

The functional analysis of students' verbal interaction focuses on the purposes for which verbal language is used in a given context. It investigates and highlights the communicative strategies applied by individual students while taking part in interaction (Halliday and Hasan, 1989). Analysis of this nature often concentrates on the illocutionary force of an utterance, that is, on its functional meaning (Austin, 1962; Edwards and Westgate, 1994). The functions for which students use their oral language are closely linked to the topic of discussion as well as to the individuals' expectations and evolving interpretations of the situation shaped by the sociocultural context of the activity. The functions of language used in the course of interaction serve both intra- and interpersonal purposes. On the one hand, the purposes and intentions carried by means of verbal language serve an ideational, i.e. cognitive, function. On the other hand, they serve an interpersonal function relating to the personal and social relationships between the interactors (Halliday and Hasan, 1989).

The identification of language functions in peer interaction takes place on the basis of implication; that is, what a speaker can imply, suggest or mean may be different to what the speaker literally says. Consequently, the functions are not identified on the basis of linguistic form. Rather, they are identified in context in terms of their retrospective and prospective effects on the actual discourse, both in terms of content and form. Data gathered by means of observations and student interviews also assists an understanding of the functions for which students use their verbal language in interaction. The functions of peer interaction are the minimum units analysed in the system. They are identified on an utterance basis and defined in terms of source, purpose and situated conversational meaning. An utterance is viewed as a meaningful unit of speech, that is, a message unit. The boundary between each utterance is linguistically marked by contextual cues. Given that an utterance may serve multiple functions, more than one function can be recorded for each utterance.

Examples of language functions we have often identified in peer group interaction across learning situations are the Informative, Expositional, Reasoning, Evaluative, Interrogative, Responsive, Organisational, Judgemental (agrees/disagrees), Argumentational, Compositional, Revision, Dictation, Reading aloud, Repetition, Experiential, and Affective functions. Some of these functions describe the nature of interaction more from the activity point of view (e.g. Dictation, Reading aloud), whereas others take a more interpretative/cognitive (e.g. Informative, Reasoning, Evaluative) or social perspective (e.g. Affective, Responsive, Judgemental) on the analysis of verbal interaction. However, none of the functions should be seen as reflecting only one of these dimensions. Conversely, each function in the framework is regarded as reflecting the social–cognitive–discursive actions of the participants as they verbally interact in their social activity. The language functions used in the course of joint problem solving often differ across situations and contexts, thus these functions presented in the analytic framework should not be understood as fixed, pre-defined categories. Instead, the functions must be situationally defined for each interaction situation on a post hoc basis.

Dimension 2: Analysis of cognitive processing

The analysis of cognitive processing examines the ways in which students approach and process learning tasks in their social activity. It aims to highlight students' working strategies and situated positions towards knowledge, learning and themselves as problem-solvers. In the method, cognitive processes are seen as dynamic and contextual in nature, being socially constructed in students' evolving interactions in the sociocultural context of activity.

In the analytical framework, we have distinguished three broad modes to characterise the nature of students' cognitive processing in peer group activity:

- *Procedural processing* refers to the routine execution of tasks without thorough planning or thinking. Ideas are not developed, rather they are cumulated or disputed without constructive judgements or criticism. The students' activity is often product oriented and concentrates on procedural handling of information.
- *Interpretative or exploratory processing*, on the other hand, refers to a situation during which thinking is made visible through language or other tools and the whole activity is focused on strategies, planning and hypothesis testing. The students' activity reflects their deep engagement and interest in the problem-solving task.
- *Off-task activity* refers to a situation during which the students' activity does not focus on the task, e.g. playing around, discussing break-time activities, 'absent minded' activity.

It is important to recognise that these three broad analytical modes are used as heuristic devices rather than distinct categories in which students' cognitive processing can be easily coded. Rather, the modes are reflected in different ways in different contexts and situations and, hence, require situational definitions.

Dimension 3: Analysis of social processing

The analysis of social processing aims to characterise the social relationships and types of participation in peer groups. The different modes in which social processing is often constructed in peer group interaction are the collaborative, tutoring, argumentative, individualistic, dominative, conflict, and confusion modes. The latter characterises interaction during which there is an obvious misunderstanding or lack of shared understanding between the children. The conflict mode reflects disagreement, usually at a social level. The dominative mode reflects the distribution of power and status in the peer group. The individualistic and dominative modes are contrasts to collaborative interaction. The individualistic mode implies that students are not developing their ideas together but rather working individually in the group. The dominative reflects an imbalance in students' social status and power. The argumentative and tutoring modes of interaction characterise the nature of collaboration between the participants. In this sense, they can be regarded as sub-modes of collaborative activity. The argumentative mode implies constructive interaction in which students negotiate their differing understandings in a rational way by giving judgements and justifications. This often leads to a shared understanding of the situation. The tutoring mode shows students helping

Table 2 Analytical framework of peer-group interaction

Dimension	Analytical category	Description
Cognitive processing	Exploratory/ interpretative	Critical and exploratory activity that includes planning, hypothesis testing, evaluation and experimenting
	Procedural/ routine	Procedural on-task activity that focuses on handling, organising and executing the task without reflective analysis
	Off-task	Activity not related to the task
Social processing	Collaborative	Joint activity characterised by equal participation and meaning-making
	Tutoring	Student helping and assisting another student
	Argumentative	Students are faced with cognitive/social conflicts that are resolved and justified in a rational way
	Individualistic	Student(s) working on individual tasks with no sharing or joint meaning-making
	Domination	Student dominating the work, unequal participation
	Conflict	Social or academic conflicts that are often left unresolved
	Confusion	Lack of shared understanding, student(s) do not understand the task or each other, often includes silent episodes
Language functions	Informative	Providing information
	Reasoning	Reasoning in language
	Evaluative	Evaluating work or action
	Interrogative	Posing questions
	Responsive	Replying to questions
	Organisational	Organising and/or controlling behaviour
	Judgemental	Expressing agreement or disagreement
	Argumentational	Justifying information, opinions or actions
	Compositional	Creating text
	Revision	Revising text
	Dictation	Dictating
	Reading aloud	Reading text
	Repetition	Repeating spoken language
	Experiential	Expressing personal experiences
	Affective	Expressing feelings

and explaining for the purpose of assisting another to understand the matter at hand. In addition, collaboration includes interaction in which participants attempt to achieve a mutual understanding of the situation, ideas are jointly negotiated, and discourse is coherent. In collaborative interaction, participants often create bi-directional zones of proximal development in assisting one another (Forman, 1989).

It must be noted that, apart from the functional analysis of peer group interaction, the unit of analysis for the different modes of cognitive and social processing is not defined by distinct rules, such as an utterance basis. Instead, the units of analysis for the modes of cognitive and social processing are based on their development in peer interaction on a moment-by-moment basis. In other respects, the three dimensions on which the analytical framework concentrates all emerge from the data as the result of the researchers' and, when possible, also the interactors' interpretations of the situation.

The categories of the analysis method are summarised in table 2. The actual qualitative description of the categories and their identification from interaction data is demonstrated via the empirical case studies discussed in part two of this book. By doing this, we want to emphasise the contextual nature of our analysis in which the analysis framework and its categories are situationally defined.

Analytical maps

In our analysis, the dynamics of peer group interaction are illustrated with the help of analytical maps, which have been created for each peer group under investigation. The product of the analysis is a series of situation-specific analytical maps that describe the sequential evolution of peer group interactions as they are constructed by students interacting with and acting upon each other's messages. In addition to highlighting the dynamics of peer interaction, these maps show the element of time in the students' activity as well as some contextual information necessary for the interpretation of the social activity in question. Although a structural map is always a simplification, it gives a coherent and temporal picture of a complex situation, making comparisons across educational contexts, peer groups and students possible. Moreover, the structural maps help one return easily to the original data to check the validity of interpretation. In addition, when presenting extracts from the data, one is able to investigate the co-text, that is, the data context to which the extract belongs.

Part II

Classroom interaction in action

Case studies of classroom talk and collaborative learning

4 Children's oral language

A comparison of two classroom organisational systems

In this chapter we give an account of a research study conducted by Fourlas (1988) in which he investigated children's roles as communicators and learners in teacher-centred and peer group-centred classrooms. An important aim of this study was to examine the influence of these two styles of classroom organisation on the ways in which students used their oral language. In order to investigate the quality and quantity of students' oral language, it was necessary to devise a system of classification that categorised language according to its function, that is, the purposes language served in a given context. None of the systems already in existence was used (e.g. Bellack *et al.*, 1966; Flanders, 1970; Halliday, 1975; Tough, 1979), nor was a new one constructed at the outset. Instead, after the data had been collected, a new, research-specific classification system was devised. As a consequence, a system of analysis emerged from the collected data, a system we have since called the Functional Analysis of Children's Classroom Talk (FACCT) system.

A functional approach to classroom talk

Oral interaction provides a rich source of data that can be investigated from many different angles. If we are interested, for example, in the purposes for which students use their oral language in classroom interaction, as well as in the social and contextual conditions in which this language occurs, a method that classifies oral interaction according to its functions appears suitable.

The functional approach to language begins by recognising its social nature, that its structures have been shaped by co-ordinating purposes and that it has developed in human societies as a potential for meaning-making within social settings (Halliday and Hasan, 1989). In viewing language as a socio-semiotic tool for expressing meanings and intentions in culture, the functional approach seems to connect closely with the sociocultural views of language and development. Both perspectives recognise the situatedness of social activity, that is, different social structures and contexts affect the nature of interaction and the ways in which language is used in a given context.

Every sociocultural context, such as a classroom with its organisation and pedagogy, has its own patterns of interaction and discourse associated with particular activity structures (Bakhtin, 1986). The existence of such stable patterns of classroom interaction enables the development of 'common knowledge' between its members (Edwards and Mercer, 1987). Learning in school, and in particular classrooms, consequently includes mastering forms of interaction and patterns of participation that are considered appropriate by the members of these sociocultural settings. It also includes learning to be attuned to contextual cues that hint towards a particular way of acting.

Another aspect of the social interaction of the classroom concerns the presence of ideologies. The social interaction of the classroom always reflects values and beliefs. In consequence, to 'talk science' or to 'talk maths' involves more than just a set of linguistic forms, it also involves learning the ideologies associated with these subjects (Lemke, 1990). This aspect becomes more clearly an issue when the academic interactions and ideologies they carry are in conflict with the student's home and community interactions (Hicks, 1995). In the functional approach, studying classroom interaction is, therefore, studying a particular discourse community in a particular social context, that is, studying the ways in which language is used and understood by the members of the classroom as well as how they participate in the communicative events they have constructed.

Despite the existence of rather stable interaction patterns present in classroom contexts, each interaction situation is still a unique and complex phenomenon. Classroom interactions are continuously negotiated and recreated – they evolve over time. The different dimensions of classroom interaction are linked not only to the historical or sociocultural context of the activity but also to the interpretations and situated meanings created in the immediate interaction context. Consequently, the nature of classroom interaction and the ways in which language is used in a given situation are also related to the participants' sociocognitive and emotional processes, including their perceptions of the aims of the activity in question (Grossen, 1994).

To investigate the dynamics and meanings of classroom interaction is extremely complex. On the one hand, there is the sociohistorical, macro-level context in which the social activity is embedded. On the other hand, there is the immediate, micro-level context, which is more fluid and evolving in nature. A functional approach to language introduces three features that characterise the relationship between language, interaction and context. The *field of discourse* reveals information about what is happening in interaction. It focuses on the meanings and contents of interaction by viewing them against the context of situation in which language is used. The *tenor of discourse* covers information about the social relationships of the participants, such as their roles and statuses. The *mode of discourse* covers information about the role of language in interaction. For example, what functions does language serve in a particular context? And what is being achieved by the use of language and particular functions?

In the light of this functional approach to language, the study described in this chapter concentrated on the mode of students' discourse in investigating the influence of two styles of classroom organisation on the functions for which students used their oral interaction. Yet, since the three features of interaction introduced by the functional approach are interconnected, understanding of one required understanding of all the others. In order to understand the functions for which students used their oral language, it was necessary to take account of the social context and conditions in which students' interaction occurred as well as to pay attention to the topics and meanings of interaction.

Background

The study sprang from a recognition that oral language, that is, the ability of children to draw upon the system of language in order to express meanings by means of speech (Tough, 1979), is essential for communication, and thus learning, in and out of school. Children and teachers use oral language for a range of purposes or functions (Halliday, 1975). These purposes reflect both the intentions of the communication and the social and cognitive processes underlying the formation and exchange of meanings in the communicative context.

In putting into operation their curriculum, teachers choose from a variety of teaching methods, each of which is founded upon particular sets of rules according to which classroom communication and interaction take place. In teacher-centred classes, that is, classes in which the children work as a single unit under the direct instruction of the teacher, the teacher tends to act like a transmitter, transmitting knowledge 'from those who know to those who do not' (Edwards and

Furlong, 1978: 28). Well-structured question-and-answer class discussion is regarded as the most appropriate route along which this transmission can take place (Sinclair and Coulthard, 1975). A 'three-fold structure' develops in classroom discourse where a teacher asks a question, the pupil answers and then the teacher evaluates the answer (Downey and Kelly, 1979: 181; French, 1987; Sinclair and Coulthard, 1975; Wells and French, 1980). A number of studies focusing on teachers' questioning behaviours during teacher-centred whole-class teaching have demonstrated that this structure limits children's participation to one third of classroom discourse time (Dunkin and Biddle, 1974; Flanders, 1970).

Discourse asymmetry exists not merely in quantity but in quality as well. The teachers' preponderance of closed and factual rather than open questions at best channels children's answers, to those expected (cf. Galton, Simon and Croll, 1980; Tisher, 1987). Yet, in evaluating children's answers, teachers give a verdict on their appropriateness and shepherd children's responses within defined limits (DES, 1975: 142). Phillips (1985) argues that the question-and-answer sequence obliges children to focus their attention on what has just been said instead of scanning across larger stretches of discourse. In that way, children probably fail to make use of contextual information in their attempt to form, interpret, understand and exchange meanings by means of oral language. In addition, it is teachers who decide what children mean or imply with what they say, which children accept, even when conscious of misinterpretation, because they are unable to prevail for long enough to make sure that their intended meaning is successfully communicated (Phillips, 1985). Therefore, teacher-centred classrooms provide a pattern of communication where 'negotiation of meaning' is constrained (Phillips, 1985: 64) and children are obliged to step into the teacher's meaning system and its frames of reference (Edwards and Furlong, 1978; Edwards and Westgate, 1987).

A 'new communication system' (Barnes and Todd, 1977: 79) takes over when teachers' authority is withdrawn by the organisation of the classroom into small groups. Group organisation frees children from the role of answerer (French, 1987), allowing them to manifest skills and competencies not common at all in teacher-dominated communication systems. By working in small groups, children are more likely to challenge and question one another, to ask for and provide elaboration, to explore and clarify ideas, concepts and meanings, to stretch their language to accommodate their own second thoughts and the opinions of others, to offer suggestions of a hypothetical nature and to reflect upon verbalised experiences (Forman and Cazden, 1985;

Phillips, 1985). Acting as senders and receivers of meanings and getting familiar with each of the participants' frames of reference, children in small groups establish intersubjectivity about the situation to which their communication refers (Wells, 1981).

Examining teacher-centred and peer group-centred classrooms

The aims of the study were to investigate the influence of two styles of classroom organisation – the teacher-centred and peer group-centred – on the ways in which students used their oral language in classroom interaction. The study was carried out in three Greek primary schools, using children aged from 7½ to 9½ years. The research sample was eight lessons, four organised on a teacher-centred basis and four organised on a peer group basis. The lessons the students were attending during the study were first language and environmental studies lessons. For each method, two teachers were observed in each of the two subjects.

The data for the study were collected and processed by means of observation, tape recordings and written transcripts. After careful examination of the data, a functional categorisation system was created to investigate the nature of children's oral language in the two classroom organisational systems.

No pre-constructed instrument was used during observations. While participating in the work of the class, the observer kept notes to provide a record of the activities and curriculum contents of each classroom and the kind of materials and information resources children were using at the time of recording. Pupil–pupil and pupil–teacher interaction, as well as turn-taking sequences in the teacher-centred classes, were also recorded by means of observation.

Tape recordings provided a permanent and full record of children's oral interaction and consequently enabled the re-examination of the data necessary for the construction of the transcripts. The intonation and volume of the speakers' voice on the tapes were taken into account in analysing the meanings and functions underlying children's language use. Constructing written transcripts was a painstaking procedure, although it proved invaluable in the functional analysis of children's talk. While reading the transcripts, the context of each child's utterance was studied in order to classify the utterance according to its function. Words, units of meaning or syntactical cues with which children organised the exchange of meanings in their talk were picked out from the transcripts, in order to use these as consistent markers for the functions identified.

The Functional Analysis of Children's Classroom Talk (FACCT) system of categorising language according to its system emerged from the collected data and, in that sense, was itself one of the findings of the study. It was essential to devise such a system because:

- currently available systems of functional analysis were limited in range;
- a pre-determined system risked limiting the categories found to those expected to be found;
- no system had been devised thus far to categorise functions of children's oral language identifiable both in teacher-centred and peer group-centred real classroom situations.

To devise and use a new classification system was not an easy task, as anyone who has worked in this area will know. This is because the meaning of one utterance clearly depended upon lengthy sections of interaction and upon the context to which each utterance referred. Therefore, it was difficult to devise sharp-cut categories. Some utterances belonged in several categories, so it was impossible to classify utterances into categories on a one-to-one basis (cf. Barnes and Todd, 1977). Problems such as these were alleviated by devising a system in which the categories were approximations. Yet, analysis of children's talk into the categories of the devised system was assisted greatly by the study of the contextual meanings, the participant observation method employed, the natural data that tape recording provides, and the identification of markers that introduce specific features in the transcripts.

Talk in the classrooms

After careful examination of the data, sixteen individual functions were identified in whole-class teaching and small-group situations, subsequently labelled as the Intentional, Responsive, Reproductional, Interrogative, Expositional, Heuristic, Experiential, Affective, Informative, Judgemental, Argumentational, Hypothetical, Compositional, Organisational, External Thinking and Imaginative.

The functions identified are briefly described below. We have also given an example of each function taken from the children's language (underlined in the talk extracts). Two things should be borne in mind, however. Firstly, the identification of each function required attention to much longer stretches of talk than can be given here. Secondly, a single utterance may be identified as fulfilling more than one function.

Intentional

This is the function of children using language to ask permission to talk, e.g.

Pupil: Miss, Miss, can I say something?
Pupil: Can I read the next one?

Responsive

This refers to talk used to respond to a question or statement, e.g.

Teacher: Do you know how the electricity is produced?
Pupil: By water.

Reproductional

Children's language was classed as Reproductional when they read aloud from a text or repeated what had recently been said by another person, e.g.

Pupil: And the ship was gone.
Pupil: The ship was gone.

Interrogative

Questions either requiring information or social approval were classed as Interrogative. There were certain features that tended to distinguish the Interrogative function in children's language, such as the use of words like 'why', 'when' and 'how'; the use of 'do' at the beginning of a sentence like 'Do you like skiing?'; and also intonation and word order, e.g.

Pupil: Why is it written with an 'o'?
Pupil: Do you want to work with me?

Expositional

When talk was used to accompany a demonstration of a phenomenon or an experiment, it was classed as Expositional. Words like
'this', 'that', 'here' and 'there' occur often in children's talk of this
kind, e.g.

Pupil:	Look. This is what I found.
Pupil:	Here are my results.

Heuristic

Children used the Heuristic function to express having found out something. This might relate to the current situation or to children's own
thoughts and ideas. The intonation in children's talk was usually
surprised, e.g.

Pupil:	Look at the way it's hanging!
Pupil:	I found that the two magnets stuck together.

Experiential

This function of oral language was used for expressing personal experiences. These were often related to children's families or personal lives at
home or school, e.g.

Pupil	My uncle used to go fishing as well.
Pupil:	So did my Dad.

Affective

The Affective function was indicated by the expression of personal
feelings and emotions. It could arise from surprise, admiration,
pleasure, amazement, disappointment, happiness, indignation and
even fear. Intonation was often a strong indicator of the use of this
function, e.g.

Teacher:	You need to have two wires and a battery. The wires are called conductors.
Pupil:	Conductors?! Like on a bus!

Informative

When a child used speech as a means of providing information, his/her oral language was classed as serving the Informative function, e.g.

Pupil: We can see fish in the first picture.
Pupil: Lots of fish with different colours.

Judgemental

The Judgemental function expressed agreement or disagreement. This could concern ideas, opinions, information or children's actions, e.g.

Pupil (reads): 'When they reached the corner, Michael began to go even faster.'
Pupil: Yes, that's good.
Pupil: No, I've thought of a better one.

Argumentational

The Argumentational function was closely connected with the use of the Judgemental function and indicated children's use of their language for reasoning and supporting their judgements, e.g.

Pupil: It has magnetic power, doesn't it?
Pupil: Yes, but the magnet must be heavier than the thing it lifts. That's the only way it can lift it.

Hypothetical

A child providing ideas or suggestions that could be used as a basis for further investigation was thought to be using the Hypothetical function. Words like 'if', 'maybe', 'suppose' or phrases like 'what about' quite often characterised the use of this function, e.g.

Pupil: What if we put it here?
Pupil: Let's do it and see what happens.

Compositional

The Compositional function referred to the use of language to create or revise a written or spoken text, e.g.

Pupil: OK. Write this down – 'How did you get here?'
Pupil: Well, you'd better say, 'How did we get here?'

Organisational

Talk used for organising work or the learning process or for controlling behaviour was classed as Organisational. Such talk often belonged grammatically to the imperative mood, e.g.

Pupil: We'll talk one at a time, OK?
Pupil: Give me that battery for a little bit.

External Thinking

When children were working at a task, they sometimes thought aloud. This kind of language was seldom addressed to anyone in particular and could easily appear as incomplete utterances, since sometimes only a part of children's thoughts were expressed in speech. There would also often be stops and starts or expressions of hesitancy such as 'er . . . ', e.g.

Pupil: And there's a boat in the picture, er . . . with a net . . .
                  er . . . in the shape of . . . what is that?

Imaginative

A child introducing or expressing imaginative situations was classed as using the Imaginative function, e.g.

Pupil: I wonder what it would be like to catch a fish that big?
Pupil: Yes, it might pull us all overboard and we'd go into the
                  sea and we'd swim to Atlantis.

Some of the labels used in this analysis system have been used by others in the past (e.g. Barnes and Todd, 1977; Halliday, 1975; Phillips, 1985; Tough, 1977). Although the terms may be the same, the meaning of the label may be different. This is because the system emerged from the collected data itself, hence each function corresponds to specific research findings.

The frequency of occurrence of these functions in the teacher-centred and peer group-centred lessons is given in table 3.

Table 3 Frequency (%) of occurrence of language functions in the talk of children in teacher-centred (TC) and peer group-centred (PC) lessons

Language function	TC (%)	PC (%)
Intentional	25.1	1.5
Responsive	28.6	2.3
Reproductional	7.6	2.8
Interrogative	7.6	3.6
Experiential	3.0	1.5
Informative	10.5	19.3
Judgemental	9.4	18.2
Hypothetical	1.1	3.1
Argumentational	2.4	7.0
Affective	1.3	4.5
Organisational	2.5	16.2
Compositional	0.6	6.1
Heuristic	0.3	4.2
Imaginative	0.2	4.0
Expositional	0.0	1.1
External Thinking	0.0	4.5

Functions such as the Intentional, the Responsive, the Reproductional, the Interrogative and the Experiential were observed to occur in higher frequencies in the teacher-centred lessons. All the other functions were found in higher frequencies in the lessons that were peer group-centred. Of further interest was the fact that children in the peer group lessons used oral language over the entire range of functions in respectable proportions. In contrast, in the teacher-centred lessons, children did not use the External Thinking or Expositional functions at all, and they used the Imaginative, Heuristic and Compositional functions quite rarely.

Talk variations across classrooms

What these children were doing with oral language in small-group and in teacher-centred lessons is clear from the results. In the teacher-centred classes, the highest frequency of occurrence was found to be the Responsive function. Although, in this study, data about the teachers' talk was not analysed, the huge difference observed between the frequency of Responsive and Interrogative functions of children's talk suggests that when children answered questions they mostly answered their teachers' questions. This concurs with the findings of other researchers, for example Flanders (1970), Bellack *et al.* (1966) and many others, and demonstrates again the role of 'answerer' that children typically play in classroom communication. From a study of the transcripts, it is clear that the children answering the teacher's recall or factual questions used the Responsive function to feed the teaching process with specific pieces of information. In this way, the teachers seemed to oblige the children to provide the classroom discourse with an expected piece of information that fitted the flow of their argument or led to conclusions they aimed to reach using their talk. Thus the teachers supervised the construction of the context to which classroom communication referred and at the same time 'helped' children to become familiar with the meaning-making system that referred to this context.

It was not the case that children in the teacher-centred classes made no initiations at all. Children using the Informative function (frequency: 10.5 per cent) provided the learning process with pieces of information that were either a personal opinion or the product of the manipulation/ description of any provided educational material. However, utterances characterised as Informative were very often followed by teacher evaluation follow-up moves (cf. Sinclair and Coulthard, 1975). From the transcripts it is also clear that many of these Informative utterances might also have been considered as Responsive, in that they were, albeit sometimes oblique, answers to teacher questions. Thus the children's initiations in the teacher-controlled communication system existing in these teacher-centred classes can be regarded rather as 'pseudo-initiations'.

In the teacherless small groups, on the contrary, children were found to make real initiations. Utterances classified as Informative were usually starting points for new episodes in the children's group discourse. In these new episodes, children often used oral language to make comments on pieces of provided information (Judgemental function: 18.2 per cent), argued for or against it (Argumentational: 7 per cent) by using previous conclusions and/or making new hypotheses (Hypothetical: 3.1 per cent). It is also quite important to note that children in these small groups providing information (Informative function), making judgements by using old and new pieces of information (Judgemental), arguing in a logical way with reference to facts and/or conclusions (Argumentational), thinking aloud (External Thinking), making hypotheses (Hypothetical) and organising the learning task by themselves (Organisational) were constructing in common a context to which the meaning of their talk referred.

One of the functions found in reasonable proportions in both classroom methods was the Judgemental function. In small groups, the children tended to judge the meanings communicated by their peers against the criterion of appropriateness to the particular task. Additionally, in group discourse, an utterance belonging to the Judgemental function was usually considered as Argumentational, Informative or even Hypothetical at the same time. This means that children judging someone else's viewpoints, ideas or actions would justify their judgements by providing arguments and alternative ideas, or even making new hypotheses to be tested. Hence, it can be argued that the children in these groups were not afraid of expressing their ideas or opinions. The Judgemental function did not operate in the same way in teacher-centred lessons. Here children made judgements mostly after having received permission for doing so, and these judgements usually consisted of only a few words. This may indicate that these children were wary of the teacher's criticism of their judgements, or simply that they had learnt the accepted rules for discourse in these classroom situations. Such judgements were not likely to be powerful enough to influence the development of the subsequent discourse.

Some important points emerge from an examination of the frequency of occurrence of the Hypothetical, Compositional, Heuristic, Expositional and External Thinking functions. These functions further indicate the existence of exploratory talk in the small-group discourse (cf. Barnes and Todd, 1977). The Heuristic function indicates the result of children's exploratory activity and/or thinking: the Expositional children's occupations with experiments; the External Thinking children's thinking aloud in search of solutions or interpretations; and the Hypothetical children's establishment of a hypothesis of which the correctness could be actively explored.

Children's identity as explorers is also suggested by the presence of Compositional function talk. This kind of talk indicates the activity of drawing conclusions, revising and presenting in oral or written form the results of children's own investigations. This function hardly occurred in the teacher-centred lessons, in which the drawing of conclusions was an activity carried out by the teacher. The teacher provided the bodies of knowledge to be learnt and the teacher revised those bodies he/she regarded as important.

Ranked third in terms of frequency in the peer group classes was the Organisational function. This stemmed from the children's roles as decision-makers. Children in the groups were responsible for deciding who should talk when, what was appropriate material to be used, what was to be done and in what ways, what the result of their work was and whether this result was good or bad, etc. (Barnes and Todd, 1977; Edwards and Furlong, 1978). In the teacher-centred classes, the organisation of the learning process, the content, the pace of learning, the information resources and the strategies to be followed were the teacher's responsibility. The Organisational function therefore occupied a limited proportion of children's talk in these lessons.

Data presented and discussed so far suggests that the teaching method had a strong influence on the range of language functions used by children participating in oral communication. It seemed, however, that within the same classroom organisational system variations in the proportions of language functions observed in different lessons might also be partly due to other factors. These factors seemed to include the sources of information available to the children and their nature, the nature of the task in hand, the nature of the provided material and the form in which children had to present their work to the class. Analysis of the influence of these alternative factors seems a promising ground for future research in this area.

Conclusions

The functions of children's spoken language were found to be restricted in quality and quantity in the teacher-centred lessons observed. The character of this teaching method, reflected in the teacher's dominance of classroom discourse, seemed to be a major factor in children's restricted use of spoken language.

The peer-group method seems to be a promising alternative that may increase the quantity and quality of children's talk. Small-group discussion would seem to have a great deal of potential in terms of children's oral language development. Its use has been explored in a variety of educational contexts, but perhaps focus now needs to be given specifically to other influencing factors, such as the nature of the group task. From this, teachers may be able to derive insights into the most appropriate ways of organising peer-group teaching methods.

5 The nature of peer interaction during collaborative writing with word processors

This chapter discusses a study that investigated the nature of students' oral language interactions during the process of collaborative writing with the computer. Specific attention was paid to the purposes for which the students used their oral language in collaborative inter-actions with their peers and how these interactions reflected their writing and learning processes. The data collection for this study was undertaken through two case studies conducted with primary-aged students. The themes of students' writing ranged from narrative texts to informative texts. The findings of this study show that the students' verbal interactions in the social contexts created by the use of word processors were highly task related, characterised by the exchange of information, questioning, judging, organising and composing. Exploratory talk and argumentative uses of language were, however, found to be infrequent, and the general nature of the interaction indicated executive and procedural activity. The implications of these findings for students' learning and writing processes will be explored in the latter part of this chapter.

Background

One of the most frequent applications of computers in primary class-rooms is the use of word processors (Blake, 1990; Koskinen, 1990). As tools with production and revision capacities, they are regarded as having a unique potential to support the aims of writing curricula with an emphasis on process (cf. Cochran-Smith, 1991; Sarmavuori, 1988). Despite the positive attitudes connected with the use of word processors, a closer look at the research on their effects reveals rather contradictory results. In some research studies, the use of word processors has been reported as changing the nature of composing processes, increasing revision and proof reading (Daiute, 1986). In others, word processing has not been found to affect composing processes in any distinct ways (Peacock and Breese, 1990). For example, no significant differences have been identified between revision done with a computer or by using pen and paper (Hawisher, 1986; MacArthur and Graham, 1987). A large number of studies have also shown that word processing has no distinct effects on the quality or quantity of students' writing (cf. Piolat, 1991). A few studies have indicated, however, that students, especially those with difficulties in handwriting, write slightly longer texts with word processors (cf. Bangert-Drowns, 1993).

In the light of this research evidence, belief in the power of word processors in writing instruction can be questioned. Yet, a closer look at research concentrating on other aspects of the educational use of word processors supports their use. A number of studies have shown that students across ability levels are motivated to write with word processors (Campbell, 1988; Haas and Hayes, 1986; Konttinen, 1985). This high motivation seems to be reflected in increased concentration spans (Blake, 1990) and in increased confidence in language skills, especially among children with learning difficulties (Daiute, 1985; Dickinson, 1986). The use of computers, together with other software like electronic mail or newspaper emulators, is, on the other hand, seen as linking students' work to the real world and, hence, increasing the meaningfulness and authenticity of writing (Campbell, 1988).

Computers are also widely thought to create a suitable environment for learning in small groups through increasing social interaction and co-operation (Crook, 1994; Jackson, Fletcher and Messer, 1992; Light and Blaye, 1990; Light *et al.*, 1987; Nastasi and Clements, 1992). Students using word processors have been found to be mutually supportive and co-operative, checking their own and each other's work, and sharing expertise (Keith and Glover, 1987). Even normally quiet or reticent students appear to participate in discussions more willingly (McMahon, 1990). In addition, students have been found to ignore adults as a source of help, starting initially to rely on themselves and one another (High and Fox, 1984). The social context created by the use of computers seems, in fact, to afford excellent conditions for collaborative modes of learning.

Investigating the nature of students' social interaction around word processors

The research reported here consisted of two linked studies, the first carried out with eight students from each school and the second with thirty students from each school. Students taking part were grouped

on the basis of their attainment levels in their first language. In both studies, the students were aged between 11 and 12 and belonged to the same type of school and class. They were familiar with each other and were used to working together during various school lessons.

In the first study, the students worked in mixed gender pairs. Eight pairs were investigated altogether. During the experiment, the whole class, including students not participating in the study, were involved in lessons using a computer. The second study involved thirty students, ten each with low, average and high attainment. There was an equal mix of boys and girls in the low attainment sub-group, but the gender of the average and high attainment students was not controlled. Thirty pairs were investigated altogether. The data collection was carried out during a lesson in their first language.

The social context of writing

The students had a set goal at the word processor: to write together in a collaborative way about topics commonly used for writing practices in their schools. In order fully to capture the nature of social interaction occurring during the process of collaborative writing with the computer, the writing topics the students worked on during the study were varied. They ranged from writing private letters to writing articles for a school magazine (e.g. horoscopes, current news, stories, factual information, how to take care of pets). In the first study, the students were given a specified topic for their writing, but in the second they were involved in making a school magazine and were able to choose the writing topic from a number of pre-selected options.

The students were allowed to devise their own ways of working at the word processor. The time allowed for writing was not set beforehand and each pair was permitted to complete their writing task. The word processing software used in each study was different but commonly used in the schools involved and therefore familiar to the students, who had used computers in their schools on a regular basis. The students' ability in using the computer and word processing software was checked before the main experiments by observing the students at work. The ways in which the students had been trained in writing skills or collaborative working skills were not examined, but it was assumed that their teachers had fostered them in their classrooms.

The oral language interactions of each pair were audio taped for about 30 minutes each. The recording started at the beginning of the students' writing, and usually the students had finished their writing task by the time the recording was finished. The audio tapes were transcribed verbatim and supplemented by field notes gathered through observations and informal interviews. The observational data consisted of information about the students' non-verbal behaviour, tone of voice, level of co-operation, turn taking, sharing the keyboard, and about the situational context in general. This information was felt necessary in order to analyse in depth the social interactions of the students. The data gathered through informal interviews consisted of unstructured questions that aimed to clarify the students' intentions and purposes underlying their talk. The questions posed to the students during the interview emerged from the situational context during the observation and, hence, were unique to each pair and student (e.g. when it was difficult to understand or hear what the child was saying, the observer asked the student what he/she meant). The informal interview took place after the students had finished their writing task at the computer.

Analysing students' social interaction

The most appropriate approach to analysis was felt to be the functional analysis system developed by Fourlas (1988; see also chapter 4 in this book). This method was selected because of its ability to give a structured overview of the nature and quality of students' oral language interactions due to its fine-grained categorisations. Table 4 gives an example of the ways in which the interaction analysis method was applied to peer interaction.

The identification of the functions from the peer interaction was carried out by the researcher alone. However, some transcripts (10 per cent), chosen at random, were double checked by a person familiar with the functional coding. Agreement between these judges reached 94 per cent.

Functions identified in the students' utterances were also coded into two broad categories: on- and off-task talk. Functions related to off-task talk are defined as talk that did not have any relationship to the writing task at the computer (e.g. 'Shall I wait for you after school?'). Functions related to on-task talk consist of talk related to the writing task (e.g. recalling experiences, general procedures or content), talk about computing (e.g. location of letters on the computer keyboard, the management of software) and talk addressed to the observer.

Table 4 The application of the functional analysis system to peer interaction

---

Context: Two girls, Elise and Madeleine, are making an imaginative story for a school magazine. They are writing collaboratively with the computer.

Elise:	let's write that one day the	(*Organisational, Compositional,*
	boys decided to go to the grave	*Imaginative*)
Madeleine:	yeah	(*Judgemental*)
	and that they took a torch	
	and some food with them	(*Compositional, Imaginative*)

Both of the students were involved in creating writing and, hence, using their talk in the Compositional function. In addition, since this was not a true story, they were imagining the situation and, hence, using their talk in the Imaginative function. Elise was also using her oral language for the Organisational function when suggesting 'Let's write . . .'. Madeleine, on the other hand, when agreeing to Elise's suggestion was using her speech in the Judgmental function. In summary, Elise used her speech for the Organisational, Compositional and Imaginative functions. Madeleine, on the other hand, used her speech for the Judgemental, Compositional and Imaginative functions.

The nature of the students' social interaction around word processors

The application of the functional coding system permitted the frequencies of each category to be calculated and, hence, compared. Table 5 shows the distribution of the language functions in the students' talk during the process of collaborative writing with the computer.

As table 5 shows, the distribution of the language functions used in the different students' talk was rather similar. The Informative function was used the most in both studies and accounted for around 17 per cent of the students' talk. The Interrogative, Judgemental and Organisational functions each accounted for around 10 per cent of the students' utterances. Although there were some differences in the use of the Compositional function in the students' talk, it still occurred fairly frequently in both groups of students. The External Thinking, Responsive and Reproductional functions covered around 5 per cent of the students' talk. The language functions occurring rarely in both studies, that is each less than 3 per cent of the total talk, were the Argumentational, Expositional, Hypothetical, Experiential, Heuristic and Imaginative functions. The Intentional function was not found in students'

Table 5 The distribution of language functions in peer interaction during the process of collaborative writing with the computer

Language function	%found in the first study	%found in the second study	%found in the two studies together
Informative	18.4	16.4	17.4
Interrogative	12.9	15.1	14.0
Organisational	10.9	14.1	12.5
Judgemental	12.0	10.8	11.4
Compositional	13.4	9.3	11.4
Responsive	7.5	7.3	7.4
Affective	3.7	9.5	6.6
External Thinking	8.1	4.3	6.2
Reproductional	6.7	5.1	5.9
Argumentational	2.8	2.1	2.5
Expositional	1.7	2.6	2.2
Imaginative	0.1	1.5	0.8
Experiential	0.5	1.1	0.8
Heuristic	1.0	0.5	0.8
Hypothetical	0.3	0.4	0.4
Intentional	0.0	0.0	0.0

interactions in either study. A closer look at the Compositional function shows that students created and dictated their writing significantly more often than they revised it.

The peer interaction that occurred during the process of collaborative writing with the computer was found to be highly task related and, to a large extent, related to writing. This suggests that the students were using the computer as a tool for their writing. They were not too involved in discussing procedural matters related to the actual use of the computer.

When looking in detail at the nature of the peer discourse, the data suggests that the students often exchanged knowledge via talk. The knowledge students exchanged in their interactions seemed to be derived not only from the school context but also from other contexts of which the students were part. This was especially apparent when the writing topic touched upon issues relating to students' life, such as their pets or recent world news.

The students were also frequently observed to negotiate their understandings about the ways they used language. Sometimes this concerned the rules of spelling; sometimes the use of coherent and understandable text. This can be seen in the following examples:

Context: Students are writing a story about the Gulf War.

Gavin:	what've they been destroying?	(*Interrogative*)
Janine:	they've been destroying houses and homes	(*Responsive, Informative*)
Gavin:	yeah	(*Judgemental*)
Janine:	let's just put houses	(*Organisational, Compositional*)
Gavin:	houses homes . . . and . . . and . . . they've been destroying factories, aren't they?	(*External Thinking, Reproductional, Informative, Interrogative*)
Janine:	yeah	(*Responsive, Judgemental*)
Gavin:	destroying . . . and all places . . . army bases've been bombed they've done . . . er . . . hmmm . . .	(*External Thinking, Compositional, Informative*)
Janine:	and . . .	(*External Thinking*)
Gavin:	and . . . er . . .	(*External Thinking*)
Janine:	D-E-S	(*External Thinking*)
Gavin:	what's that . . . hmmm . . .	(*External Thinking, Interrogative*)
Janine:	D-E-S, D-E-S . . .	(*External Thinking*)
Gavin:	they've been destroying army b . . . posts . . . boxes . . .	(*Compositional, Reproductional, External Thinking*)

Context: Students are writing about dogs.

Christian:	let's write about the different kinds of dogs . . . let's write that there are many breeds and . . . hmm . . . the most common breed in Finland is a Finnish spitz	(*Organisational, Responsive, Informative, Compositional, External Thinking, Informative, Compositional*)
Melanie:	what's the most common breed	(*Interrogative*)
Christian:	the most common breed in Finland is a Finnish spitz . . . Finnish spitz	(*Responsive, Reproductional*)

Melanie:	oho . . . can I do it like that . . . put it like that (using the keyboard)	(*Heuristic, Interrogative*)
Christian:	it's a small-sized, reddish hunting dog	(*Reproductional, Compositional, Informative*)
Melanie:	small . . .	(*Reproductional, Interrogative*)
Christian:	sized	(*Responsive, Reproductional*)
Melanie:	reddish	(*Reproductional, Interrogative*)
Christian:	hmmm	(*Responsive, Judgemental*)
Melanie:	reddish fur	(*Reproductional, Interrogative*)
Christian:	hunting dog	(*Responsive, Reproductional*)
Melanie:	what . . . hunting dog	(*Reproductional, Interrogative*)
Christian:	hmm . . . what breed is your dog	(*Responsive, Judgemental, Interrogative*)
Melanie:	we've had a dog . . . we haven't got a dog at the moment	(*Responsive, Informative, Experiential*)
Christian:	what breed	(*Interrogative*)
Melanie:	golden retriever	(*Responsive, Informative*)
Christian:	we've got a Leonberg . . . it'll grow very big . . . it's a puppy now . . . it's stupid	(*Informative, Experiential, Affective*)
Melanie:	haha . . . what'll we write next	(*Affective, Interrogative*)
Christian:	how about our dog	(*Responsive, Interrogative*)
Melanie:	okay	(*Responsive, Judgemental*)
Christian:	my dog is	(*Reproductional*)
Melanie:	should I put that Christian's dog is	(*Compositional, Responsive, Interrogative*)
Christian:	well, yeah . . . its breed is Leonberg	(*Responsive, Judgemental, Reproductional*

Questioning was also frequently found in the students' discussions. They often, for example, used their oral language to acquire information about correct spellings. Sometimes, while creating the plot for their writing, they asked for each other's opinions and ideas about objects, persons and events. Hence, through questioning, the students appeared to use each other's cognition to solve problems they were facing in the course of writing. In addition, they seemed to use questioning as a means of recalling their own knowledge and understanding.

Context: The students are writing for a school magazine. They are writing a horoscope.

Elise:	what was it?	(*Interrogative*)
Hanna:	for human beings	(*Responsive, Compositional*)
Elise:	a horoscope for human beings	(*Reproductional*)
Hanna:	yeah	(*Judgemental*)
Elise:	shall I write it together . . . horoscope . . . no . . . wait . . . shall I write it like that?	(*Interrogative, External Thinking, Organisational, Interrogative*)
Hanna:	hahhah . . . cap (reading aloud the spelling mistake in the word 'horoscope')	(*Affective, Reproductional*)
Elise:	I think it should be written together	(*Informative*)
Hanna:	no	(*Judgemental*)
Elise:	horoscope . . . of course you write it together. Shall I write – you can compare human beings to real scorpions. They can be as dangerous . . . hah . . .yeah . . . human . . . beings . . . shall we put that? *Do I write scorpion with a capital? It's an insect.*	(*Judgemental, Informative, Compositional, Interrogative, Informative, Affective, External Thinking, Interrogative, Interrogative, Informative*)
Hanna:	yeah	(*Responsive, Informative*)
Elise:	Can I spell it like that? then . . . the scorpion can be compared with . . . I think we should write that human beings	(*Interrogative, Compositional, External Thinking*)

should be compared with real
scorpions . . . human beings . . .
human . . . beings . . . we could
put that . . . human beings . . .
should I put that human beings
and scorpions . . . how
could I . . .

It is interesting to note from the data that the amount of questioning in the students' talk was significantly greater in frequency than that of replying. The reasons for this may have been due to the students' inability to provide answers to questions. Yet the transcripts suggest that the students required not always information or help from their peer but just social approval. Moreover, sometimes the students asked questions to recall their own knowledge or to think more deeply about the contents of their writing. Questioning of this form did not necessarily require a verbal response. Students also sometimes answered questions through non-verbal behaviour, for example by pointing out the answer from the text on the computer screen. In the light of these observations it seems, in fact, that the students also tried to create intersubjectivity through means other than the use of oral language.

The students were frequently found to use their oral language for expressing agreement or disagreement during joint writing at the computer. Thus they seemed to be actively involved in judging and criticising their work. They did not, however, often give justifications for their arguments and easily accepted each other's judgements. In consequence, argumentative discourse was rare in their conversations.

Context: Students are writing a letter to a boy in Africa. They are describing winter.

Donna:	what shall we write to him? shall we just . . . shall we just put 'How are you?' or something?	(*Interrogative, Responsive, Organisational, Compositional, Interrogative*)
Owen:	are . . . I spelt it right . . . didn't I?	(*Reproductional, External Thinking, Interrogative*)
Donna:	haha	(*Responsive, Affective*)
Owen:	how are you (reads the screen)	(*Reproductional*)

Donna:	question mark. How can you start to tell about the snow? Here it's snowing. Come on	(*Organisational, Informative, Interrogative, Compositional, Informative, Organisational*)
Owen:	all over England it's snowing	(*Informative, Compositional*)
Donna:	yeah . . . now go down	(*Judgemental, Organisational*)
Owen:	it's snowing rapidly	(*External Thinking, Compositional*)
Donna:	hmm . . .	(*External Thinking*)
Owen:	how do you spell it	(*Interrogative*)
Donna:	R-A-P-I-D-L-Y . . . full stop. What's the weather like in Africa?	(*Responsive, Informative, Reproductional, Organisational, Compositional*)
Owen:	we can write that in the end . . . can't we?	(*Organisational, Judgemental, Interrogative*)
Donna:	yeah	(*Responsive, Judgemental*)
Owen:	We have to explain everything first. When we've said it's snowing rapidly over in England we can't start to talk about something else.	(*Organisational, Judgemental, Informative, Argumentational*)
Donna:	What can we write then?	(*Interrogative*)
Owen:	In the snow you'll become soaking wet or at least last night when I was out with the boys I did become soaking wet.	(*Responsive, Compositional, Informative, Argumentational, Experiential*)

The nature of the interaction suggests that organisation was a common feature of the students' writing processes. The students were often found to organise their writing turns at the computer. In addition, they wanted to organise the theme, contents and surface-level features of their writing (e.g. the order of words or letter size).

Context: Students are writing jokes for a school magazine.

Felipe:	you should've written the name	(*Informative,*
	Marne with a capital. Is it	*Interrogative*)
	followed by a question mark?	
Melanie:	come on . . . write more	(*Organisational*)
Felipe:	we should've put a full stop	(*Argumentational,*
	there	*Informative,*
		Organisational)
Melanie:	do it then	(*Organisational*)
Felipe:	it's your turn to tell a joke	(*Organisational*)
Melanie:	but I can't think of any	(*Informative*)
Felipe:	so . . . what is . . .	(*External Thinking,*
		Compositional)
Melanie:	let's write a quiz	(*Organisational*)
Felipe:	don't interrupt me	(*Organisational*)
Melanie:	oh, no	(*Affective*)
Felipe:	haha	(*Affective*)
Melanie:	well . . . let's take it away	(*Organisational*)

The students were also often observed, unsurprisingly given their task, composing writing in their discussions. They negotiated the style, content and technical features of their writing and, hence, collaboratively explored new ways of expressing themselves. In addition, while dictating, the students often showed a willingness to share the writing task with their peer.

Context: Students are writing about the recession.

Melanie:	let's start writing	(*Organisational*)
Felipe:	the recession is causing	(*Compositional,*
	pressure	*Informative*)
Melanie:	how could we	(*Interrogative*)
Felipe:	the recession is causing	(*Responsive,*
	pressure . . . hah.	*Reproductional,*
		Affective)
Melanie:	the recession has hit our	(*Compositional,*
	school	*Informative*)
Felipe:	huh (looks puzzled)	(*Affective*)
Melanie:	let it be as it is	(*Organisational*)

Felipe:	okay . . . there	*(Judgemental,*
		Informative)
Melanie:	what then	*(Interrogative)*
Felipe:	the recession has hit . . .	*(Responsive,*
	(interrupted by Melanie)	*Compositional)*
Melanie:	no . . . the recession has hit	*(Judgemental,*
	the teachers . . .	*Compositional)*
Felipe:	the teachers of our St. Jo's	*(Compositional)*
	school (uses the nickname of	
	the school)	
Melanie:	our St. Joseph's school . . .	*(Compositional)*
Felipe:	so that the skirts of the	*(Compositional,*
	teachers have gone shorter	*Imaginative)*

A closer look at the use of the Compositional function reveals that revision was not a common feature of the students' writing processes. Moreover, when it occurred it mostly concerned minor, surface-level corrections, like the changing of words in a sentence or spelling corrections. Revisions concerning bigger-structural changes were rare in their discourse.

While reproducing written or oral text, either by reading or repeating, the students seemed to be involved in considering other possibilities for the contents of their writing. They were reminding themselves of what they had already written and what they were thinking of writing next. Moreover, they were checking the correctness of their writing or demonstrating a mistake in it.

Context: Students are writing a horoscope.

Alicia:	let's write one more and then	*(Organisational,*
	make another title. This is the	*Compositional,*
	worst month of the year.	*Imaginative)*
Raphael:	yeah, hahah	*(Judgemental, Affective)*
Alicia:	hahah so this is the worst	*(Affective,*
	month of the year . . . full	*Reproductional,*
	stop . . . shall I now read this	*Organisational,*
	aloud	*Informative,*
		Interrogative)
Raphael:	yeah	*(Responsive,*
		Judgemental)

Alicia:	this week something terrible will happen to you especially at home and in the shops you'll make a fool out of yourself . . . in the banks you'll stammer. You'll need to visit the doctor every day . . . this month is the worst one of the year	(*Reproductional*)
Raphael:	put . . . (interrupted)	(*Organisational*)
Alicia:	should we put a full stop there (refers to the text just read aloud)	(*Organisational, Interrogative*)
Raphael:	yeah . . . do that	(*Responsive, Judgemental*)

The students also used oral language as a means of thinking aloud while composing or when writing text into the computer. This kind of language use was seldom addressed to anyone in particular. In addition, it often sounded unfinished, since the students expressed only a part of their thoughts in speech.

Context: Students are writing a horoscope.

Alicia:	your father . . . father . . . hahah . . . how could you say it? Well . . . your sisters make faces at you.	(*External Thinking, Compositional, Interrogative, Compositional, Imaginative*)
Raphael:	yeah	(*Judgemental*)
Alicia:	your sisters and brothers brot . . . her . . . s . . . I was just about to do that	(*Compositional, External Thinking, Informative*)
Raphael:	shall we write more	(*Interrogative*)
Alicia:	what then? Your father starts to listen to the music of the 60's . . . haha	(*Interrogative, Responsive, Imaginative, Compositional, Affective*)
Raphael:	yeah	(*Judgemental*)
Alicia:	no, we can't do that since not all students have a father . . .	(*Judgemental, Argumentational,*

no, your mother starts . . .	*Hypothetical,*
starts . . . to wear a mini-skirt	*Informative,*
	Compositional,
	Imaginative,
	External Thinking)

Although the External Thinking function was often expressed with grammatically incomplete sentences or words, the data suggest that it served an important role in the students' writing process. The use of this function appeared to help the students to control their own actions, create ideas and solve problems.

The occurrence of the Expositional, Heuristic, Hypothetical, Experiential and Imaginative functions were found to be low in the students' conversations. Thus exploratory discussions were fairly rare. The Intentional function was not found to occur at all in the students' conversations. The implications of these findings are discussed in the following sections.

What do these findings suggest about the nature of the students' social interaction?

The results of this study imply that not only did the students use the computer as a tool for their writing but they also employed another valuable device to help them in their joint writing task. This was their oral language. The data show that the students often used their oral language for exchanging and acquiring information. In sharing their understanding through oral interaction, the students were able to make connections between their own and their partner's knowledge and to explore issues mutually. This may have made it easier for them to construct new notions that went beyond their individual level of understanding and, hence, helped them to work in their zone of proximal development (Vygotsky, 1978).

Moreover, when receiving information, the students were able to compare it to their own pre-existing knowledge. If this information was in disagreement with their own understanding, they had to resolve this conflict. This may have affected the students' cognitive structures and processes (Doise and Mugny, 1984; Nastasi and Clements, 1992).

The high amount of questioning in the students' conversations suggests that the students relied on themselves as information sources and that they were trying to create a mutual understanding of their writing at the computer. Wells (1987) sees the use of the Interrogative and Responsive functions as giving evidence of students trying to build intersubjectivity in their discussions. This is widely considered to be highly significant in terms of students' joint meaning-making and learning (Brown and Palincsar, 1989; Feldman, 1990).

The occurrence of the Organisational function suggests that the students were in charge of their work at the computer. Furthermore, the expression aloud of working and writing strategies may have given the students opportunities to self-monitor their activities and possibly their own cognitive functioning. These are all important acts in the process of developing writing and learning skills (Bereiter and Scardamalia, 1987; Brown, Armbruster and Baker, 1986).

The occurrence of the Judgemental function in the students' interactions gives evidence of the students having been in charge of their working and writing at the computer. This is an important condition for effective learning (Butterworth and Light, 1992; DeCorte, 1990). A closer look at the students' talk shows, however, that the students seldom justified their arguments. In consequence, reasoning and argumentation were rare in these students' conversations. Yet, engaging in the argumentative use of language is highly valued in education (Cohen, 1994; Jackson, Fletcher and Messer, 1992; Mercer, Phillips and Somekh, 1991; Phillips, 1990). This is because its use is seen as assisting students to think, justify, evaluate and reformulate their understanding and opinions.

The high occurrence of the Compositional function in these students' talk strengthens the assumptions that hold that word processing encourages students to think about their writing and to attend to the meaning of it (Adams, 1985; Kahn, 1988). The observation of their low revision behaviour also supports other research findings on collaborative writing with computers, which have reported students to focus mostly on the surface-level corrections without paying much attention to bigger, structural revisions of their text (cf. Cochran-Smith, 1991; Hawisher, 1989).

It has been suggested that the reasons for students' low revision behaviour at the computer are due to the limited screen size and the neatness of the text produced (Chandler, 1990). Recent research findings imply, however, that students' revision behaviour is related to their writing manner and skills rather than to the actual use of the word processor. Revision behaviour has not been found to change in any significant ways between handwriting and word processing (Hawisher, 1986; Peacock and Breese, 1990).

The occurrence of the Reproductional function in these students' talk indicates intensive task involvement. In addition, it implies that they were interested in their joint writing at the computer. Other researchers (Daiute, 1986; Davies, 1989; Pearson and Wilkinson, 1986) have also reported that word processing encourages students to read their writing from the computer. This is thought to be due to the fact that the text on the computer screen is fairly easy for all students in the group to read and see at the same time (Kahn, 1988).

Talk accompanying the students' writing appeared to be not only addressed to a peer but also used for controlling and directing their own thinking. The occurrence of the External Thinking function appeared, in fact, to reflect the students' self-guidance, since they were able to help themselves by means of oral language. Vygotsky (1978) sees a constitutive function in monologue. This is because he considers egocentric speech to be a stage of transition from vocal to inner speech, from speech for others to speech for oneself. Bruner (1990) also sees an important function in monologic narrative in terms of assisting students' cognitive development.

The use of content-free tools such as word processors can be viewed as creating a learning context that encourages students to learn as a process of exploration and discovery (cf. Cochran-Smith, 1991). Although this might be true, this form of behaviour was not found to be reflected in these students' oral language interactions in any significant ways. Hence, exploratory discussions were rare. From the data, it appears that the occurrence of the Expositional and Heuristic functions was very low in the students' talk at the computer. The Hypothetical, Experiential and Imaginative functions also did not often occur in the students' interactions. Yet, their importance in fostering learning is widely recognised (Cohen, 1994; Edwards and Mercer, 1987; Mercer, 1994; Phillips, 1990; Wells, 1987). Exploratory discourse can be seen as increasing students' awareness of those strategies needed in the process of problem solving, which include writing.

It is important to acknowledge that, although verbal interaction can play an important function in collaborative writing with computers, it is not the only means, and the findings of this research demonstrate this. For example, the non-existence of the Intentional function in the students' conversations and the unequal number of questions and answers appeared to be due to the fact that the students also communicated with each other in non-linguistic ways. Furthermore, the students seemed to communicate via the computer screen by reading each other's texts. The occurring text on the screen may thus have played a role in the students' social construction of writing.

The meanings and functions underlying students' social interaction are embedded in broader sociocultural contexts (Rogoff, 1990; Vygotsky, 1978; Wertsch, 1991). There are the histories of individual students, the history of a certain group, the task presented to the students in the group and the social setting of the classroom and of the whole school. Beyond these there also lies the wider context of the society of which the school is a part. Consequently, the nature of peer interaction during the process of collaborative writing with the computer is strongly embedded in its broader sociocultural context as well as in a situation-specific context (Crook, 1994).

The present research, conducted in two different cultural contexts, suggests that the peer interaction that occurs during the process of collaborative writing with the computer can play an important role in the students' social construction of writing and learning. Through peer discourse, these students seemed to take an active role in applying, constructing and discovering their knowledge. Furthermore, while communicating their ideas about writing, they were able to become aware of their peers' as well as their own thinking and writing processes. All this may have fostered the students' metacognitive awareness (Bereiter and Scardamalia, 1987; Brown, Armbruster and Baker, 1986). It also seems, however, that the nature of students' oral language interactions during the writing process tended to be fairly procedural and executive in nature, with limited presence of argumentative discourse.

The findings of this study imply that, although the context of collaborative word processing can create excellent opportunities for collaborative modes of learning by fostering interaction between students, this context does not automatically encourage students to justify their arguments, make hypotheses or, in general, explore the learning context. In order to encourage students to use their language for reasoning and exploration, it is important that attention be paid to the classroom learning context as a whole. This includes the role of teachers in helping students to acquire skills needed for effective interaction and learning.

To improve the quality of interaction in the word processing context, more emphasis needs to be placed on teaching students the skills linked with effective interaction and learning. Students should be made aware of the strategies needed for effective writing and learning. Recent research has already provided evidence that training students in collaborative learning skills can foster their use of explanations during collaborative problem solving (Repman, 1993). Word processing software with educational prompts could also encourage students to reason and explore their ideas and strategies in the production of their writing. A closer investigation of aspects such as students' ability, gender and interpretation of the situation during collaborative writing with the computer would also help educators to give their students better opportunities for learning in the social context created by the use of word processors.

6 Children's talk in an early years classroom
Leadership and control

The study reported in this chapter was designed partly to illustrate the insights that might be gained from the use of the functional analysis of classroom talk system to investigate the social interaction of an early years classroom. A particular focus was to explore the ways in which the various leadership roles adopted by children during collaborative work were signalled in their uses of talk. What follows is an outline of how the study was conducted, including details regarding the school context, the nature of the tasks recorded and brief profiles of the children. The process of analysis is then described and the language functions observed are quantified.

Background

Teachers rely heavily on observation as a basis for their assessments and judgements of children's social and academic competence. However, these assessments are inevitably based on intuitive and subjective interpretations of what is happening. In a recent study by Bennett, Wood and Rogers (1997), teachers of young children identified informal observation as their primary mode of assessment and talked of the important role of 'gut feelings' and 'intuition' in making judgements about children's development. Clearly, such intuitive observation is an important aspect of early years teaching and should not be undervalued. In research also, particularly in the early years field, observation is the leading method of inquiry, perhaps because of its strong links with the scientific practices of child development. It is possible, however, that as a result of an overdependence on observation alone, certain assumptions about children, particularly about their facility for productive social interaction, have come to be taken for granted in some quarters. Therefore, an analytic system that can either challenge or validate our intuitive knowledge about children is to be welcomed.

The context of the study

This case study was carried out with children aged from 7 to 8 in a small primary school in the southwest of England. Three classroom activities were recorded and subsequently analysed. These were planned by the class teacher with two requirements: one, that they should involve work in three different curriculum areas and, two, that they should involve children in collaborative work. The children being studied were used to working independently from the teacher and with each other in groups based on a range of ability, friendship and the nature of the task. For the purposes of this study, children were selected at random. Each group consisted of four children of similar age and ability but of mixed gender. The following offers a brief description of each task.

Activity 1

The purpose of this activity was for the children to investigate the effects of adding water to sugar, salt and rice. A series of questions given on a prepared sheet asked children to record, in writing, their predictions and actual outcomes based on observation. Although they were asked to work collaboratively, each child had an individual recording sheet to complete.

Activity 2

Here, the focus was on map skills within the class geography topic on the local area. Once again, the children were asked to answer the questions on a prepared sheet. As in activity 1, each child had an individual sheet on which to write his/her answers.

Activity 3

In this maths activity, the children had to throw three dice 50 times and record the totals. The teacher had previously undertaken a preliminary activity with the class and shown them ways of recording their results in a grid. They were asked to produce jointly a similar grid in which to show their results and identify patterns of frequency.

Profiles of children

In the following, we will provide a few details about each of the children involved in the study. These are, of course, rather superficial, but they may help to put the activities into context.

- Lucy is a very vocal member of the class. She reads fluently and her spelling is extremely accurate for her age. She is rather bossy and impatient at times, although she is a well-liked member of the class.
- Ella is a bright and lively personality but, at times, rather anxious about her work. She reads and writes well, although she is rather disorganised – if not chaotic – and her work is generally untidy. Ella can be rather volatile and argumentative, but is a popular member of the class.
- Elizabeth is very able, a fluent and expressive reader who also writes well for her age. She is usually quiet, but self-assured.
- Gavin is also very able in all areas of the curriculum. He can be rather nervous and his speech tends to be rushed and, therefore, difficult to follow. However, what he says reflects a good grasp of ideas and sense of humour.
- Christopher is extremely able, intellectually mature and possesses an impressive general knowledge. He is regarded by other children as clever – the 'professor' – and is frequently consulted on matters relating to work.
- Clair is very able, reads well, although she has some difficulty with spelling. She is generally very quiet, even reticent, in class.
- Gwilym is a complex character who questions everything before accepting it – the class sceptic! His reading and writing are not as developed as some other children, but intellectually he is quite a sophisticated thinker.
- Brett is highly competitive and, at times, can be rather serious. He is a good all-rounder and reads well for his age.
- Mark is new to the school, but has quickly established himself as a prominent member of the class. He is bright and keen, with a sunny disposition. He reads and writes well and can be highly articulate.
- Amy is quiet, but self-possessed. She is good at reading and writes with flair and imagination.
- Lynne is very quiet and rather unassuming. She works quietly and demands little attention. She reads and writes well for her age.

It is important to note that the researcher involved in this study also taught these children on a part-time basis. Thus interpretations of their language and behaviour are quite likely to have been shaped by the researcher's knowledge and perceptions of them as learners and individual personalities. On the other hand, the dual perspective of teacher/researcher may be advantageous in making sense of contextual factors, in particular the impact of group characteristics on children's interactions.

Observing and investigating the social interaction

The children's performance of each activity was recorded on both audio and video tape. Given the critical importance of contextual factors in the analytic process being used in this study, it seemed that the use of the video would provide a more permanent record of the activities and enable repeated observation. The talk used during the activities was transcribed initially from the cassette tapes. However, some practical problems emerged during this process. Firstly, it was not possible to distinguish from the cassette tape the gender of the child speaking; nor was it clear who was actually speaking at any particular time. Secondly, close observation of the activities on video revealed that a significant amount of talk had, in fact, been omitted completely or misheard. To rectify this, the transcripts were extensively revised and expanded from the video material, a process that proved to be a useful precursor to a more fine-grained analysis of the texts where contextual clues such as intonation and gesture could be noted.

There was no perceptible reaction from the children to the video camera during the recording, and, while it is impossible to be certain about this, it seemed that their language was, for the most part, unaffected by the presence of the researcher and/or the recording tools. The researcher deliberately did not interact with the children during the activity, and the children did not approach her at any time. In two of the three activities, the class teacher intervened to check progress and respond to a question from a child. However, his interactions were brief on both occasions and, as such, did not appear to influence substantially the course of either activity. In light of this, the analysis does not take the teacher's interventions into account.

The point was made in the introduction that observation of children can lead to informal judgements about what is going on. It is important to note at this stage that observing each activity (albeit through the lens of a video camera) did leave the researcher with some powerful impressions of what was happening, about who was in control of the activity, about roles adopted and, moreover, about how successful it was in terms of the collective and individual experience.

Applying the functional analysis system

The transcripts were read several times for meaning before the process of identifying language functions commenced. Where ambiguities seemed to exist, the video material was consulted for contextual clues. Functions were identified within each language utterance and checked 'in context'. Most language utterances utilised multiple rather than single functions. The following extract, taken from activity 2, illustrates this.

Lucy:	Isn't it EE3?	(*Interrogative*)
Christopher:	No, it doesn't look like we've got the grid reference. Yes we have, up here. So its DE3. No, No, it says here, look, Holy Cross. It's F1. F1 is somewhere round here.Well, here's Holy Cross Church. Can you see, Gwilym? Can you see East Town?	(*Judgemental, Argumentational, Heuristic, Expositional, Interrogative*)
Lucy/Gwilym:	Yes.	(*Judgemental*)

The video material was an invaluable source of information at this stage. It enabled the complexities of children's interactions to be better understood through constant reference to intonation, gesture and action.

The analytic process

Identifying functions was by no means a mechanistic process. It was a challenging and sometimes difficult process necessitating a continuous sifting through the data for contextual clues. It was during this process that the researcher's impressions of the activities began to make sense, as certain functions became associated with individual children. Thus, identifying functions was a highly interpretative process, where the functional analysis fused with information derived from observations.

In the course of the analysis, patterns began to emerge across activities. For example, in each observation clear leaders emerged at the outset and remained largely unchallenged by other members of the group for the duration of the activity. In the analysis, leadership became closely associated with the use of the Organisational, Judgemental and Argumentative functions of language. In addition, styles of leadership varied and could be explained in terms of the way in which children used certain functions. A fuller discussion of this is given below.

Insights into the nature of the children's social interaction across tasks

Although each activity lasted for about 25 minutes, activity 2 produced significantly more language utterances (307 in total) than either activity 1 (156) or 3 (146). Table 6 shows the range and spread of language functions utilised in each activity. Several issues emerge from this data that seem of particular interest.

The use of the Reproductional function

The figures for the Reproductional function show a significantly higher use in activity 2 – a total of 31 instances, compared with 9 and 2 in activities 1 and 3 respectively. Although each activity required the children to read questions from a sheet, activities 1 and 2 had more questions than activity 3. However, this cannot account for the high number of instances of Reproductional language in activity 2.

Table 6 Language functions used in each activity and across activities

Language function	% in activity 1	% in activity 2	% in activity 3	% in all activities
Intentional	2.5	2.5	1.2	2.1
Responsive	0.5	1.7	1.2	1.1
Reproductional	8.0	13.1	4.9	8.7
Intentional	2.5	2.5	1.2	2.1
Responsive	0.5	1.7	1.2	1.1
Interrogative	15.2	14.3	9.8	13.1
Expositional	7.1	2.5	4.3	4.6
Heuristic	1.0	2.7	1.2	1.6
Experiential	0.0	0.0	0.0	0.0
Affectional	0.0	3.0	0.0	1.0
Informative	10.6	11.0	8.6	10.1
Judgmental	21.7	23.4	14.1	19.8
Argumentational	8.6	6.7	4.3	6.5
Hypothetical	3.5	1.0	4.9	3.1
Compositional	0.0	1.7	0.0	0.6
Organisational	15.2	7.1	23.3	15.3
External Thinking	3.0	3.4	19.6	8.7
Imaginative	0.0	1.5	0.0	1.5

Sometimes the children used this function while map reading. For example:

Lucy:	Isn't that where it says, er,	(*Interrogative,*
	'Crediton Parish Church'?	*Reproductional*)
Lynne:	Yes. It says 'Holy Cross'	(*Judgemental,*
		Reproductional)

However, examples that can be specifically linked to the task of map reading are relatively few. More frequently, children used this function in episodes of text construction and in reading back their own writing. When they were engaged in the process of both writing and reading aloud, as in the following extract, the Reproductional function was linked with External Thinking.

Lucy:	What are we writing?	(*Interrogative*)
Gavin:	'Go along' A – L, errm	(*Reproductional,*
		External Thinking)

One possible explanation for this is that the children in activity 2 engaged in more frequent and sustained episodes of sharing of ideas, spellings and joint construction of writing. By contrast, in activity 1, although the nature of the task was similar, the children tended to work on their sheets individually. This is an important possibility that needs to be taken into consideration when planning for collaborative work in classrooms. A number of research studies (e.g. Bennett and Dunne, 1992; Galton, Simon and Croll, 1980) have suggested that simply sitting children in groups does not guarantee that they will work collaboratively.

The use of the External Thinking function

There was a striking variation in the proportion of utterances suggesting External Thinking across the three activities. In activity 1, 3 per cent of utterances were classified as having this function, with 3.4 per cent in activity 2. In activity 3, however, 19.6 per cent of utterances were classified as showing External Thinking.

One could speculate that this suggests a marked task effect in terms of the language production of these children. Both activities 1 and 2 were, although ideally collaborative, possible for the children to complete without really interacting that much. Activity 3 demanded collaboration in that it asked for a joint outcome. It was also the only one of the three activities overtly open-ended in its demands. There was no guidance given on what the children were to find in their investigation, whereas in activities 1 and 2, the children were given prescribed formats for recording what they found.

External thinking through the medium of language is a highly prized use of language in the theoretical literature on verbal interaction. These findings confirm others' suggestions that, to ensure this use of language, a great deal of attention needs to be given to the nature of the tasks asked of children.

The question of leadership

In all three activities, the predominance of the Judgemental, Argumentational and Organisational functions was striking. These three functions were mostly used by children who adopted the leadership role within the group. The following data demonstrate the extent to which this was the case.

The use of the Judgemental and Argumentational functions

There appeared to be a close relationship between these two functions and they frequently appeared in the same utterance. Consider, for instance, Ella's use of each function during activity 1. Of the 43 total uses of the Judgemental function, 18 were made by Ella, 7 of which were used in conjunction with the Argumentational function (this function was only used 17 times in total in this activity). Although Ella did not emerge as the clear leader of the activity, she made several attempts to assert herself and argue her point of view. The data suggests that the use of the Judgemental and Argumentational functions were her major linguistic tools for doing this.

The use of the Organisational function

On the individual level, the distribution of these functions was particularly interesting. In activity 1, 17 out of a total of 30 uses of the Organisational function came from Lucy. In activity 2, 25 out of a total of 29 came from Christopher and in activity 3, 24 out of a total of 38 came from Brett. This in itself is perhaps not surprising: by definition, leaders organise and control the behaviour of others, although they may achieve this in quite different ways. But what was surprising was the extent to which such functions dominated the language of individual children.

Uses of the Interrogative function and its relation to styles of leadership

The analysis identified two distinct uses of this function. The first was specifically related to seeking reassurance. Elizabeth, in particular, used language in this way when she was unsure and perhaps concerned that she might be wrong. For example:

Lucy:	. . . secondly, now the sugar.
Ella:	The sugar Elizabeth, Elizabeth's doing the sugar.
Elizabeth:	How much? *(This could be simply seeking information, although her intonation suggested an element of seeking for social approval.)*

And later:

Elizabeth:	. . . It's not enough, it's not enough, is it? *(Again, there was an element of seeking approval here.)*

The children were writing up their observations of the experiment. Although they had been asked to work collaboratively, they wrote independently from one another. Elizabeth's tone of voice and behaviour indicated that she was unsure of what to do.

In the following extract, Elizabeth was asking for information, although put in the wider context of the activity her tone of voice indicated that her intention was to seek reassurance.

Elizabeth:	Lucy, are you going to write on the sheet?
Lucy:	I don't know.
Elizabeth:	How much have you done?
Lucy:	I've finished.
Elizabeth:	Do you have to write on the sheet, it says 'fill in the sheet'.
Lucy:	No, no, no, no, no silly!

The transcripts were littered with examples of this kind. Identifying the appropriate function relied heavily on not only intonation and gesture but also on an understanding of the activity as a whole.

Analysis revealed a possible relationship between the use of the Organisational function and Christopher's use of the Interrogative function. Although, like Elizabeth, he used language of this kind in order to seek approval, the intention underpinning this was quite distinct. In several cases, he used this kind of question as an organisational device, one that moved the action on and served to keep the group together. The way in which he did this was impressive. In this way, he demonstrated sophisticated interpersonal skills. He elicited the participation of other children, yet retained control over the activity at all times.

This can be compared with the talk of Brett in activity 3, whose mode of leadership lacked sophistication. He adopted a rather more authoritarian approach. His use of the organisational function was blunt and to the point. He gave orders rather than options.

Brett:	Yes. So, we get started. Which idea shall we use? Shall we go and get all the equipment?	(*Judgemental, Organisational, Interrogative*)
Brett:	We'll stick these two pieces together. *(demonstrating)*	(*Organisational, Expositional*)
Mark:	. . . at the bottom, so we'll get another piece . . . we can cut that bit off.	(*Organisational*)
Brett:	We'll sellotape this.	(*Organisational, Expositional*)
Mark:	Right, we'll write the numbers down.	(*Judgemental, Organisational*)
Brett:	. . . write the numbers down.	(*Reproductional*)
Mark:	This way, up to 20?	(*Interrogative*)
Brett:	Yes, 20. That way. Then we'll do a few lines . . . Yes. Who wants the next go, writing and drawing?	(*Judgemental, Expositional, Organisational, Interrogative*)
Amy:	Me.	
Brett:	Then we'll do lines. You do down 25 and across 20. Yeah. No, not like that, do a line, but underneath all that.	(*Organisational, Expositional, Judgemental*)
Mark:	Do you want me to get a ruler?	(*Interrogative*)
Brett:	Yes. . . . It's straight up. Move it across a bit that way. Make sure it's 25.	(*Judgemental, Organisational*)
Mark:	Up to the end of the ruler nearly.	(*Informative*)

Although he accommodated Mark, Brett's approach effectively excluded Amy and Lucy from the activity altogether. They remained at the margins and were virtually silent throughout. Their acquiescence was total as they became passive recipients of instructions given by the two boys. Gender clearly played a part in the outcome of this activity, although not exclusively. Other factors such as personal characteristics may also have been influential. However, the degree of domination exhibited by Brett and, equally, the unassertive behaviour of Amy and Lucy were surprising and would not have been predicted from knowledge of these children. The functional analysis strongly supports these comments. Of a total of 148 language utterances during this activity, only 9 came from Amy and 9 from Lucy. These figures are quite striking and provide evidence to support subjective interpretations of the activity.

This analysis raises some serious issues regarding grouping practices. In classrooms where children work in fixed groups, it is critical that teachers are alive to the dynamics of the group, in order to ensure that children's learning and social experiences are, for the most part, positive and productive.

Functions not present in the children's talk

In addition to the Responsive function, which has already been discussed, examples of the Experiential, Imaginative and Compositional functions were conspicuously absent from the data. How can we account for the clear contrast between the figures for these and, say, the Judgemental function?

Some significant factors may be group size and the nature of the tasks, in particular the requirement for children to collaborate. Analysis revealed a high frequency of Organisational, Judgemental and Argumentational functions. In the earlier discussion, these were clearly linked to leadership. Following on from this, it may also be that in group work situations, children may spend much of their time organising the activity and their relationships, rather than attending to the task itself. On the basis of this study, it could be argued, therefore, that group work leads to predominantly socially oriented language and that the functional analysis system has the capacity to provide evidence of this. Promoting social development is, of course, valid in educational terms, but may raise questions concerning aims and objectives for learning.

The nature of the tasks may explain the absence of language associated with creative activities, such as imaginative role-play, story writing and so on. There was little scope for this in the activities. Only Christopher utilised the Imaginative function as he tried to conceptualise walking down the roads on his map. It may also be true that children generate a wider range of language functions in paired work, where organisational issues may be less of a concern and where sharing and negotiating roles is easier. These comments are, of course, speculative, although it is clear from what has emerged so far that an analysis system that allows a close and systematic look at children's language in the context of their activities is of great potential use to both teachers and researchers.

7 The dynamics of peer interaction in a geometrical problem-solving task

In this chapter we will discuss a case study that investigated the nature of students' social interaction while working in dyads on an open geometrical design task in an elementary classroom. The goal of this study was to highlight how social interaction between the students' supported and challenged collaborative reasoning in a less structured problem-solving situation. In addition to characterizing symmetric and asymmetric peer interaction and considering the reasons for them, the study pays attention to the elements in the social learning situation that appeared to create conditions for collaborative and exploratory learning in mathematics.

Background

Within mainstream thinking in education, following social constructivist theorising, it has become common to ask, 'What challenges does a view of cognition as a socially shared, situated activity pose for instructional settings and pedagogical activities?' Equally, it has become important to rethink the methodological tools that are used to untangle the complexity of situated social activity and its connection to instructional goals. Despite contemporary views of the social nature of learning, it appears that learning in instructional settings is still often conceptualised as an individual activity. In many cases, the nature of knowledge is understood as a conceptual system to be transmitted to the learner. Furthermore, instructional settings do not seem to take account of the learner's conceptual frameworks. Mathematics education seems to be no exception to these general facts of life in real classrooms (O'Connor, 1998).

In the study reported in this chapter, the conceptual structures of the learner and of the mathematics to be constructed were not seen as two distinct systems to be linked through artificial pedagogical means.

Here, the instructional setting provided students with opportunities to elaborate and reorganise their knowledge and understanding, rather than simply applying and acquiring cognitive structures and procedures. In this learning context, the students' implicit conceptions of spatial understanding worked as a starting point for the development of their geometrical understanding.

The goal of the study was to investigate the situated dynamics of peer-group interaction while pairs of students solved design problems in geometry. Of particular importance were the conditions for and mechanisms of collaborative interaction in peer interactive pairs. The analysis of the students' joint problem solving focused on the processes and forms of their joint meaning-making while negotiating their interpretations of the relevant construction principles of solids. Attention was also paid to the ways in which the students' verbal interactions reflected their mathematical understanding and geometrical thinking.

Description of the learning situation

The learning situation in which the students worked in this study was designed in collaboration between the research team and a classroom teacher, and it was related to the students' current curriculum work in mathematics. The actual learning situation did not, however, follow the traditional pedagogy of mathematics but was rather based on pedagogy that stresses the learner's conceptual framework and social activity in the construction of mathematical thinking (Kaartinen, 1995). This pedagogy draws on sociocultural approaches to learning and development (Brown and Renshaw, 2000; Wells, 1999).

The design task allowed students to approach the learning situation in multiple ways by posing problems and sub-problems as heuristic devices. The evaluation and negotiation of the strategies and approaches were carried out in pair groups, and the task allowed the students to reorganise and elaborate their conceptual understandings, with the inclusion of everyday and mathematical explanations. From the mathematical point of view, the goal of the design activity was to involve the learner in a learning situation in which mathematical theory might be constructed by negotiation and experimentation (Lemke, 1990). Semiotic tools and social activity play an important role in this meaning-making process.

In the actual design task, the students were asked to construct three-dimensional objects pictorially represented on a plane with the help of two-dimensional objects. The construction was carried out using cards representing different faces of objects. The pictures of the geometrical objects could be visualised in different ways, and hence there were many solutions.

The goals of this task contrast with traditional approaches to mathematics education, which implicitly hold an assumption that mathematics, including geometry, is learned as an organised conceptual system from axioms to theorems and to conclusions. In this design problem, the learners' task was to make sense out of a chaotic reality by choosing appropriate activity patterns from several possibilities. The appropriate activity patterns included posing relevant problems, constructing and evaluating working strategies and, in the case of social activity, negotiating a joint language or, more accurately, a joint working space with a partner.

Investigating the social and cognitive dynamics of peer interaction

Altogether, twenty 12-year-old students from one primary classroom participated in the study. The data collection was conducted in four sessions each lasting between 25 and 45 minutes. Each student participated in all the sessions by engaging in design tasks in geometry. The first and the fourth sessions consisted of solo activity, whereas the design tasks in the second and third sessions were solved in pairs. This chapter concentrates on the data obtained from the pair sessions.

Each session of group problem solving was video taped as a whole and supplemented with the researchers' field notes. In addition, the students answered a questionnaire that aimed to shed more light on their collaboration, their attitudes towards the tasks and their perceived goals. Stimulated recall interviews were also held with each student individually in order to clarify their orientation, working strategies and understanding of the concepts dealt with within the task, as well as to increase understanding about the nature of their collaboration and interaction. Such a triangulation of research methods was considered necessary to increase the validity of interpreting the dynamics of social activity within peer groups.

The data were analysed in several phases. In the first phase, the video material of the students' social activity was examined together with the field notes written down during observations. Next, the verbal interaction of the pairs was transcribed, the questionnaires encoded, the students' work assessed and the interviews summarised. After that, the interaction and behaviours apparent in the video tapes were analysed with the help of the analytical framework described in chapter 3. In the analysis, particular attention was paid to the nature of the students' verbal interactions and their cognitive and social processing. Other features observed and analysed included the students' use of the instructional tools available in their problem-solving situations (e.g. texts, cards, images, etc.) and their construction of time and task within their activity. The data analyses were revisited in the light of the contextual knowledge acquired through observations, stimulated recall interviews and pre-study teaching experiences in the classroom. The data were collected and analysed by two researchers together. Disagreements concerning the analysis of peer interaction were negotiated among members of the research team until joint agreement was established.

Examples of symmetric and asymmetric interactions

In the following, the results of the study will be highlighted by two cases representing the social activity of two pairs: Alex and Maria (case 1) and Jon and Tim (case 2). Case 1 highlights the processes of symmetric interaction, whereas case 2 illustrates asymmetric interactions between the students. In summary, the cases reveal micro-level process information about the situated dynamics of peer-group interaction within the context of the design task. In addition, they highlight the students' geometrical thinking in the process of joint meaning-making. For this chapter, situational process data were considered more informative than generalised findings across the complete data sample collected in the study.

Case 1: Symmetric interaction

Table 7 shows the interactive dynamics of a pair of students, Alex and Maria, during their work on the design task. The social activity of the pair was highly collaborative, including tutoring and argumentative episodes during which the students helped one another, usually by explaining their points of view through verbal and non-verbal interaction, as well as with the help of the tools they were using. The cognitive activity of the pair, during which strategies and solutions were jointly created and tested, reflected intensive task engagement and was very exploratory in nature.

As can be seen from the transcript in table 7, Alex's first question (turn 125) reflects the students' attempts to create a joint meaning for the problem to be posed. In his turn, Alex questioned Maria's idea of the structure of the solid to be constructed. Maria, in response,

Table 7 Interactive dynamics between Maria and Alex

SESSION: 1.1.2 Mathematics
STUDENTS: Maria and Alex
WORKING TIME: 09:09–09:23

Time	Participation		Transcribed peer interaction	Language functions	Cognitive processing	Social processing	Contextual notes
09:18	125	Alex	Bottom . . . how come	argumentative question	speculating	collaborative	solving task no 6
09:19	126	Maria	no . . . but that's the bottom . . . that's that sort of a triangle and the lid is that sort of a triangle . . . they are connected . . . it shows there how they are connected	answering by demonstration	explaining	collaborative tutoring	
	127	Alex	no . . . look . . . this is	arguing			
	128	Maria	yeah . . . its connected	arguing			
	129	Alex	wait	organising			
	130	Maria	that could be created by side triangles in a way	reasoning	speculating		
	131	Alex	triangle comes here . . . triangle comes here . . . triangle comes here and here comes a rectangle	demonstrating	explaining		outlining the geometrical object

Time	Turn	Speaker	Utterance				
	132	Maria	yeah . . . exactly and here to the roof as well	agrees and reasons			Maria tries to speak at the same time
	133	Alex	could it go here	reasons	speculating		
	134	Maria	this one . . this one yeah . . . wait a minute . . .yeah this is the rectangle	reasons	testing		
	135	Alex	and this belongs to there too	reasons			
	136	Maria	should we find another one similar to that	reasoning question	proposing strategies		
	137	Alex	like this	answering by reasoning			
	138	Maria	no it's smaller	argumentation			
	139	Alex	it's smaller . . . there . . . no it isn't	agrees and reasons			
09:20	140	Maria	no it isn't . . . .what if that bottom is different . . . let's take these bigger ones you suggested . . . since these are of equal size here at the back . . . now I found another one . . . . the little triangles go there . . . . the little long ones go	agrees, organises, and reasons	exploratory solving	collaborative	

seemed to approach the problem-posing from the mathematical structure of the task. Alex's following turn, 127, shows that the students had not yet created a joint problem space. The reason for this could lie in the fact that Alex's sketch of the solid was different from Maria's. On the other hand, Alex's comment could reflect problems in conceptualising the situation from Maria's point of view. Turn 131 suggests that the students had now created a joint understanding of the situation. From the mathematical point of view, Alex led Maria's thinking further (see turn 126) by explaining the form of the side face of the solid to be constructed. Consequently, from the mathematical point of view, turns 126 and 131 seem to be essential for the construction of joint problem space.

When investigating the nature of the mathematical language the students used in their interactions, it appears that they conceptualised the structure of the solid from the holistic point of view by using universal concepts of mathematics (see e.g. turns 126 and 131). The construction process of different faces of the solid shows, however, that the students were creating situated meanings when describing particular elements of the faces to be constructed. For example, they talked about small, long and large triangles when selecting from many potential possibilities. In terms of the task, one might expect to hear such items of mathematical language as equilateral, isosceles, scalene triangles and so on.

The analysis of the whole data of the dynamics of Maria's and Alex's interaction shows that the pair's social activity was composed to a great extent of task-oriented problem solving including organising working processes and exploratory activity, characterised by intensive negotiation and high-level reasoning of the problems encountered. Also, many speculative episodes were found in which the students were doubtful about the solution or the opinions of their partner. These speculative episodes were often followed by testing episodes, during which solutions and opinions were tried out. The social interaction of the pair was coherent and highly collaborative, reflecting mutual understanding and equal participation in problem solving. The collaborative nature of the interaction was also highlighted by tutoring and argumentative episodes, during which the students were helping one another to grasp their way of thinking and understanding. The quality of the pair's work was also assessed to be high: 11 points out of 12.

The analysis of these students' verbal interactions revealed that the pair's interaction was mostly characterised by the Reasoning, Judgemental, Organisational, Argumentative, Evaluative and Demonstration functions. In the flow of student interaction, the use of these functions often resulted in Reasoning, Argumentational and Organisational episodes.

There were slight differences between the students' communicative strategies. Whereas Alex seemed to agree more often with the ideas and suggestions created (Alex used the Judgemental [agreement] function 39 times as opposed to Maria's 21), Maria was more involved in reasoning (88 to 39), organising (49 to 21) and evaluating (19 to 10). These differences may be partly explained by Maria's somewhat greater subject knowledge, as assessed by the classroom teacher. Yet, as shown by the other data, the differences in the students' communicative strategies seemed not to hinder the pair's problem solving or collaboration.

The data gathered by means of student questionnaires and interviews support the researchers' interpretations of the nature of peer interaction. Both students considered their collaboration to have gone very well and felt that their joint work made problem solving easier. The students also considered that they had not faced any problems, that the quality of their problem solving was high, and that they had learned from each other. Also, the goal of the exercise had been understood by both in the same way. Interestingly, both students thought the goal of the exercise was related to the development of concentration skills. This finding seems to reflect the fact that the students do not necessarily conceptualise such learning situations as promoting mathematics learning, since the situations differ markedly from their regular mathematics learning in the school context.

Case 2: Asymmetric interaction

Table 8 shows the social activity of another pair, Jon and Tim, also working on the design task. The social interaction of this pair was quite different to that of the Alex/Maria pair. Here there was a marked imbalance in the students' collaboration and joint problem-solving. As the extract shows, Jon seemed to dominate the activity in social and cognitive terms. Although at the beginning Tim was eagerly involved with the task, Jon's domination gradually affected Tim's working processes and participation, leading to signs of a 'free-rider effect'.

In this extract, Jon asked Tim to find a large triangle. Tim seemed to agree with this by responding with an affective statement, although his attention was directed to holding the cards the students had already constructed. Jon continued his orders but did not explain what he

Table 8 Interactive dynamics between Jon and Tim

SESSION: 1.1.2 Mathematics
STUDENTS: Tim and Jon
WORKING TIME: 11:05–11:30

Time		Participation	Transcribed peer interaction	Language functions	Cognitive processing	Social processing	Contextual notes
11:16	147	Jon	where is the large triangle?	asking for information Q(I)	looking for a face	slight domination from Jon's side	students are trying to find correct faces to construct the geometrical object
	148	Tim	oh, yeah . . .	affectional utterance (AF)	Tim is holding the construction students have already made		
	149	Jon	take those away	organising (OR)			
	150	Tim	hahah . . . what are you looking for?	affectional utterance (AF) and asking for information Q(I)		Tim initiates collaboration	
	151	Jon	a kind of a triangle to the center . . . these tasks are a bit too difficult.	answering A(I) and evaluating the task (EV)	explaining		

	Speaker	Utterance	Coding	Process	Comment
152	Tim	how about this one then?	reasoning in a question form Q(RS)	speculating	
153	Jon	it might be ... perhaps two of these there ...	reasoning (RS)		
154	Tim	basically no	reasoning (RS)		
155 11:17	Jon	show me ... hmm ... let's turn to the next exercise ... let's solve that one since it is easier ... it is what one sees ... hey, could it be these ...	organising (OR), evaluating (EV), and reasoning (RS)	organising working, speculating	slight domination from Jon's side
156	Tim	do you mean these small ones?	reasoning in a question form Q(RS)		Tim initiates collaboration
157	Jon	these	answering A(RS)		
158	Tim	what about these big ones, I think they look big ... like this.	reasoning (RS)	speculating	
159	Jon	I think ... (indistinct)	–		
160	Tim	I don't know ...	informing (I)		signs of 'a free rider effect' starting to appear

Table 8 continued on next page

Table 8 (continued)

Time	Participation	Transcribed peer interaction	Language functions	Cognitive processing	Social processing	Contextual notes
161	Jon	that's a bit too thick that one there . . . that's there . . . rather small . . .	reasoning (RS)	comparing cards		
162	Tim	that's not it . . . heheheh	reasoning (RS)			
163	Jon	its all the same really	reasoning (RS)			
164	Tim	let's try both	organising (OR)			
165	Jon	let's take . . . this is there below, isn't it? . . . bigger one . . . hold it	organising (OR), reasoning (RS), and organising (OR)	organising working		
166	Tim	no, I don't want to	disagrees (Jd)		social conflict	

was actually trying to do. Tim tried to ask Jon to clarify his thinking and strategies, but Jon seemed to be thinking aloud rather than aiming towards joint problem-solving or understanding. This lack of shared understanding can also be seen in the pair's incoherent verbal interaction (e.g. conversational turns 152–155, 158–161). The lack of argumentation and explaining episodes in this peer interaction further suggests the imbalance in the students' social activity.

The mathematical language of this pair did not reflect a holistic perception of the problem posed. Instead, this pair seemed to approach the task from particular features (compare turn 126 of case 1 to turn 147 of case 2). Pair 1, Maria and Alex, started their activity by defining the joint problem and negotiating a joint interpretation of the situation. This may have been a conscious strategy to construct collaboration or a more implicit one created in the process of social activity. Pair 2, on the other hand, seemed not to aim for collaboration and joint meaning-making. At least the students did not make their problem posing explicit, to be shared with a partner. The mathematical language of the pair reflected a disintegrated system of geometry. The problem space seemed to be merely constructed of triangles of varying size. The conceptualising of the situation remained at the level of everyday descriptions and was not linked to mathematical language. This conclusion is supported by the fact that the students too, in their interviews and questionnaires, expressed the need for more support from a teacher to help them in their task.

The analysis of the complete dynamics of Jon's and Tim's social interaction shows that at the beginning the students were task oriented and interested in the design task. Both students started the activity eagerly. Soon, however, Jon started to dominate the task, for example by handling the cards and giving orders, and did not give Tim much space. Tim did not seem to notice this at first but gradually started to be a bit restless when his ideas or suggestions were not taken up by Jon. Interestingly, Tim soon accepted his role and started to withdraw from the activity, letting Jon do most of the problem solving. From the data it appears that Jon was rather thinking aloud than trying to solve the design task collaboratively. Only in those instances when Jon regarded the task as difficult to solve did he start to seek confirmation of his ideas from Tim. The quality of the pair's work was average: 7 out of 12 points.

The functional analysis of these students' verbal interaction shows that this was mostly characterised by the Reasoning, Organisational, Questioning and Affective functions. As with pair 1, Reasoning and

Organisational episodes reflected the nature of the design task, which seemed to encourage exploratory activity.

The results show that Tim produced more affective statements than Jon (65 to 34). Jon, on the other hand, organised the activity (98 to 40) and reasoned (116 to 70) more frequently than Tim. The differences in the students' communicative strategies and types of participation demonstrate further the imbalance in the students' social activity. In addition, they highlight differences between the students' subject knowledge and social behaviour. Tim's subject knowledge in mathematics was assessed by the classroom teacher as being much lower than that of Jon.

The data gathered by means of student questionnaires and interviews give slightly different interpretations of the nature of peer collaboration and joint problem solving than those derived from observations. According to the students, their collaboration was good and pair group work made problem solving easier. Yet, the students expressed the view that they had not learned anything from each other and that they would ideally have liked some help from the teacher. There were also differences between the students in their interpretations of the task goals. Tim considered the goal of the design task to be related to the development of concentration skills, whereas Jon thought they were related to mathematical thinking. Again, this finding may be explained by the students' unfamiliarity of working in the mathematics learning situation designed for the present study.

Learning geometry in collaborative interactions

A traditional view of mathematics education would emphasise the role of definitions, theorems and proofs as a basis for knowledge construction. The universal language of mathematics creates a common ground for meaning-making, and fluency in this language is, in general, a condition for becoming a member and an active participant of the scientific community (Lemke, 1990; Wertsch, 1991). It is, however, somewhat misleading to think that mathematical regularities could define the processes of learning (Vinner, 1991). Traditional pedagogy in mathematics education often holds that mathematical concepts should be transmitted to the learner by means of definitions that are then later used in solo problem solving. Such problem solving allows for the integration and practice of newly learned concepts.

In the study described in this chapter, the pedagogical approach to the teaching of mathematics was to engage the learner in social activities designed to encourage collaboration, negotiation and the social construction of geometrical thinking, mediated by the semiotic tools provided by the activity setting. What mattered here was to activate learners' conceptual frameworks in posing problems and seeking explanations from an open and multi-faceted learning situation. In this learning context, we hypothesised that there would be a dynamic interplay between everyday and mathematical explanations while different voices were participating in social activity in order to construct a common ground for meaning-making. Within the context of the geometrical design task, these voices reflected different approaches to space, varying from practical to universal.

The data suggest that the instructional setting in which the students worked in this study encouraged intensive task-engagement, collaboration and exploratory activity, including reasoning and problem posing and solving. The students' verbal interactions showed evidence of hypothesising, reasoning, argumentation, organising and questioning. These are all important features of effective interaction and provide opportunities for the social construction of knowledge (Cohen, 1994). In addition to verbal language, the cards representing shapes of plane geometry seemed to be appropriated by the students as cultural tools to assist their thinking and joint understanding. Consequently, the social context in which the students worked provided students with different means to create a joint working space. Features such as the complexity and openness of the task, student initiation in meaning-making, and the opportunity to use everyday knowledge in problem posing and solving seemed to create enabling conditions for joint construction of mathematical thinking. Moreover, the opportunity to be able to continuously monitor their success in solving the design problems seemed to promote the students' motivation and task involvement. In particular, the visualisation made possible by the use of pictures, cards and joint language seemed to make continuous monitoring and evaluation possible.

In contrast to the traditional view of mathematics education, these findings suggest that everyday meanings and metaphors are important resources for joint understanding and conceptual learning (Moschkovich, 1996). Rather than emphasising the limitations of everyday language in comparison to the universal mathematical language, it seems more important to recognise and appreciate the value of everyday voices in orchestrating mathematical explanations and understanding. The purpose of mathematics education in modern society is, after all, to provide the means to succeed rather than the means to fail.

The open and complex nature of the design task was reflected in different forms of collaboration and diverse cognitive approaches. On the basis of the data, it appears that the students used relevant features of the solids as heuristic devices during the sketching process, despite the fact that they were not yet aware of the nature of the solid to be constructed. Although the students' verbal interactions during the problem solving did not reflect a great deal of mathematical terminology, they appeared to create relevant situated meanings that scaffolded their thinking about the properties of mathematical solids. On some occasions, the discussion was occupied with situated meanings that the students jointly created in the course of their interaction, despite the fact that one of the students in the pair group did seem to be able to use universal mathematical concepts. Consequently, the logic of students' interaction and the conceptual meanings it carried were reciprocally established in the students' evolving interactions shaped by the social and cognitive dimensions of their activity.

The data also reveal differences in the students' collaborative relationships: true collaboration, including argumentation and tutoring, led to sophisticated solutions, whereas competitive or dominative interaction seemed to hinder joint problem posing and solving. Particularly in pair groups in which power and knowledge were not equally distributed, the outcome was in some cases asymmetric interaction and problem solving, diminishing the potential for collaborative learning. On the other hand, in some cases these situations resulted in peer tutoring episodes or argumentative episodes during which the more knowledgeable member of the pair scaffolded his/her partner towards a joint understanding and meaning-making.

In summary, the social and cognitive dynamics of peer-group interaction appear to be important and yet very complex elements of peer-group learning. This challenges the methodological approaches that are typically used to investigate collaborative peer-group interactions and learning processes. It is evident that the methodological tools need to take a more dynamic and process-oriented approach to social interaction and learning. In addition, they should recognise the role of physical and psychological tools in shaping the nature of social activity. On the whole, there is a need for multi-layer analyses that support one another and that enable investigations of the relationships within and between them. Analyses of this nature are likely to increase current understanding of the social conditions and practices of collaborative learning and how they mediate individual growth.

The study suggests, on the whole, that small-group design tasks based on complexity and openness can give students opportunities for joint construction of mathematical understanding, geometrical sketching and spatial thinking. Moreover, the possibility to link every-day experiences with the conceptual language of mathematics seemed to help students to take responsibility and to be involved in their learn-ing. Yet, attention has to be paid to the situated dynamics of student interactions and collaboration in order to ensure that social activity leads to personal growth. The pedagogical challenge suggested by this study is to consider how situated meanings created in peer inter-actions could be scaffolded towards a universal conceptual language of mathematics.

In the future, it seems important to investigate the role of the teacher as a designer of learning situations and as a participant in student-initiated collaborative meaning-making. The present study as a whole provides some guidelines for these issues. Close, micro-level analysis of peer interactions highlights the nature of students' conceptual expla-nations and the problems that emerge in joint problem solving. This information provides the basis for future design and implementation of learning situations. For example, in the present case, the next exer-cise for these students could be related to classifying plane shapes and negotiating joint universal meanings for them. In these instruc-tional situations, the teachers' role would be to guide students' situated, everyday explanations towards universal ones while still valuing student initiation and language.

8 The nature of students' social interaction and information processing in a multimedia-based learning situation

This chapter describes a case study that investigated the instructional setting and students' learning activity in one elementary classroom using multimedia CD-ROM encyclopaedias for their science learning. Particular attention was paid to the students' sociocognitive processes and constructive activity while handling and processing the information from multimedia-based science material in a small-group poster task.

Learning and instruction in the age of information

Recent endeavours in educational reform, shaped by economic and social developments, have posed new requirements in classroom instruction. This has included rethinking the goals of instruction and the means that are used to achieve them. In addition to critical thinking, problem solving and the collaborative learning skills emphasised in instruction today, technological changes and developments have also posed new requirements for the learning skills needed in the twenty-first century (Bransford, Goldman and Vye, 1991; Goldman, 1997). Among others, these skills include the ability to handle and process information from multiple sources within and across different media (Rouet et al., 1996; van Oostendorp and de Mul, 1996). On the whole, it appears that the design of instructional situations that support the development of the skills required in the coming era is a challenge for current educational research and practice.

A typical feature of classroom instruction following recent technological and social developments is the use of project- and problem-based learning activities that emphasise collaborative learning in authentic situations, the active construction of knowledge in social interactions with peers and experts, goal-directed information search processes and synthesising across multiple sources. These activities are also located in technology-based learning environments, which have been shown to have the potential to support authentic and meaningful learning in learning communities (Scardamalia and Bereiter, 1996). In addition to many developmental research projects that have specifically created and developed technology-based learning environments for meaningful, collaborative learning (e.g. McGilly, 1994; Wilson, 1996), classroom teachers in more traditional schools are also facing the introduction and uptake of new media together with modified conceptions of learning and instruction. Many schools have made substantial investments in computer hardware and software and are expecting teachers to use them in their instruction across the curriculum. Unfortunately, in many cases too little attention is paid to the instructional quality of the software or to the pedagogical practices in which technology is used. How technology-based instruction is actually carried out in traditional classrooms, and what learning experiences these practices give rise to are, consequently, important questions to be researched.

Background to the study

The processes involved in technology-based learning and instruction have been approached and explained with reference to current views of learning and development, based on constructivist and sociocultural perspectives. These views define knowledge as a dynamic and complex entity that is not something objective existing outside the individual, but which is constructed through individual thinking, socially distributed processes and cultural activities (Salomon, 1993). Accordingly, learning is seen as a knowledge construction process that is linked to the learner's sociocognitive frameworks and to the sociocultural context of activity (Resnick, 1991).

Constructivist views emphasise the active role of the individual as a constructor of knowledge. Consequently, meaningful learning is regarded as taking place not via knowledge transmission but rather via knowledge building mediated by socially distributed processes (Resnick, 1991; Salomon, 1993). According to the constructivist perspective, active, goal-directed information exploration and striving towards understanding, which Scardamalia and Bereiter (1993) call *intentional learning*, is segregated from procedural learning and its coincidental outcomes. According to this line of thinking, significant components regulating learning processes are found in individuals' conceptions of the nature of knowledge and learning, in the subject-related knowledge base, and in mindful and goal-directed information-seeking behaviour and reflective activity, including the use of appropriate learning strategies, such as cognitive and metacognitive strategies (Pressley and McCormick, 1995; Vosniadou, 1996; Young, 1997).

Sociocultural views of development have directed attention to the social and situated aspects of knowledge as well as to the role of culturally formed semiotic tools in mediating constructive learning activity (Vygotsky, 1978; Wertsch, 1991). From the sociocultural point of view, learning is an enculturation and meaning-making process that occurs through participation in cultural, dialogic activities with peers and more knowledgeable members of the culture (Rogoff and Toma, 1997; Wertsch, Hagström and Kikar, 1995). Of particular interest from this perspective are the nature of social activities and participation structures that members of the learning community engage in during joint meaning-making and knowledge construction. What has also become significant from this perspective are the cultural values, norms and rules that regulate learning activity and define what counts as knowledge and knowing under certain circumstances (Kumpulainen and Mutanen, 1999).

In the light of current views on learning, it seems crucial that classroom instruction aims to support learners' active participation and engagement in knowledge construction and communal thinking (Goldman, 1997). This can be achieved by creating meaningful and motivating learning activities in which learning material is presented in authentic and multiple forms and which promote formulation of representations and explanation, as well as communal sharing and knowledge building via different mediating tools (Vosniadou, 1994).

Multimedia – possibilities for instruction and a challenge for the learner

In addition to the necessity to provide students with adequate skills to apply and use information and communication technology in their everyday lives, there is evidence to suggest that technology has the potential to support learning by creating inherently challenging, meaningful and motivating instructional situations (Wilson, 1996). Technology appears to provide a stimulating and supportive context for collaborative small-group interaction and learning (Kumpulainen, 1996; Mercer, 1994) as well as multiple possibilities for information presentation, distribution, exploration and construction. Moreover, it allows information to be presented in holistic, complex and networked forms, as it is typically encountered in natural and authentic situations. Different applications of technology can model and simulate complex problem-solving situations and, with different tools, assist learners to link the information at hand to their conceptual frameworks (Spiro *et al.*, 1991). This can be realised, for example, by creating representations and explanations in multiple formats via multiple channels in a socially shared learning activity.

The variety of technological applications used in educational contexts is extensive. Among the most recent innovations in education is the use of computer-based multimedia. Examples of the commonly used multimedia applications in most elementary classrooms are CD-ROM encyclopaedias, often used as information resources for different kinds of inquiry and/or project-based learning activities. Such computer-based electronic encyclopaedias are a typical representative of interactive multimedia, which present information through hypertext structures in the form of text, sound, still or animated graphics, and film segments.

The advantages of multimedia over more traditional tools can unquestionably be found in its facility to present a vast amount of information at reasonable cost, and in its developed search functions (Megarry, 1988). From the educational point of view, the open learning environment created by multimedia promotes, it is claimed, intensive task-engagement and exploration (Perzylo, 1993). The different channels and structures through which information is presented, such as hypertext, sound, graphics, animations, charts and video clips, are thought to support authentic and meaningful learning, allowing many different strategies to be used in the access and handling of information. This supports current conceptions of effective learning that emphasise real-world complexity and the unstructuredness of many knowledge domains. The networked structure of multimedia is even said to model experts' semantic knowledge structures and, thus, to help the novice to learn not only the information at hand but also the expert's knowledge structures (Jonassen and Wang, 1993). Yet, although the complex and networked nature of knowledge may support current conceptions of learning and instruction, there is a danger that the pedagogical context in which multimedia is used might encourage learners to process multimedia-based information in a transmission mode, for example by memorising the material. Moreover, multimedia in itself is unlikely to support learners' intentional regulation of their cognitive activity by means such as monitoring, reflecting and controlling their own strategic actions.

Despite its potential to support authentic, problem-based and student-sensitive learning, it is evident that multimedia in itself cannot produce revolutionary effects on learning. Processing information in the multimedia context requires active, goal-oriented information-seeking behaviour on the part of the learner (Lawless and Brown, 1997). This includes guiding and monitoring one's own navigation and making relevant choices while moving in the networked environment. The learner must continually be able to evaluate the meaningfulness of the information presented, consider where to move next and conceptualise holistic entities from discrete pieces of information (Hammond, 1993). The sheer amount of information, the hyperlink structures linking it together and the freedom to move autonomously in the material all create pressures for goal-directed information handling and processing activity, especially on novice users. Tergan (1997) and Oliver and Oliver (1996) refer to this problem using the term *additional cognitive load,* which does not only cause problems in handling and processing multimedia-based information, but can easily distract the learner's attention from relevant information.

The use of dynamic cognitive strategies has been reported to be significant particularly in complex learning situations, such as while working in multimedia-based learning contexts (Goldman, 1996). Typically, research into the cognitive strategies used in multimedia-based learning contexts has concentrated on describing students' navigation strategies (e.g. Barab, Bowdish and Lawless, 1997; Perzylo, 1993; Wright, 1993), despite the fact that strategies are complex in any cognitive activity comprising different activity patterns. In addition to navigation strategies, multimedia environments embody strategies related to reading, writing and information processing. These different strategies become extremely important when the user's responsibility in handling complex data increases (Foltz, 1996). Information handling, critical evaluation and selection become especially important (Lehtinen, 1997).

It appears on the whole that handling and processing multimedia-based learning material requires the highly active use of diverse cognitive skills and strategies that are related to efficient information seeking, processing parallel pieces of information, note making, organising, associating and evaluating information and detecting incoherence (Goldman, 1997). In the light of these requirements, intentional learning can be even more demanding in multimedia environments than in more conventional learning situations.

Investigating learners' use of multimedia

This study and its methods were grounded in the constructivist and sociocultural perspectives to learning and instruction. The focus of the study was on evidence that could highlight the nature of students' sociocognitive and constructive activity in a multimedia-based science learning environment. Micro-level on-line analyses were used to investigate students' discursive, cognitive and collaborative activity while handling and processing information from a multimedia CD-ROM science encyclopaedia.

In this study, sociocognitive activity was defined as a dynamic and contextually embedded process that mediated and regulated learning. From this point of view, sociocognitive activity was comprised not of simple strategic procedures but rather of heuristic and complex activity patterns embedded and shaped by the sociocultural context.

The study involved eighteen 12-year-old students from an elementary classroom working individually and in pairs on a poster task. The classroom in which the study took part was special in that it was equipped with modern observation technology enabling effective collection and analysis of on-line data.

The multimedia software

The multimedia software used in the study was the *Encyclopaedia of Science* (Dorling Kindersley 1996) CD-ROM, which covers topics in mathematics, physics, chemistry and life sciences. The interface of the software consists of the *Console* page (the main page), the *Subject Topic Menu* pages and the *Article* menu pages, through which topics can be found according to their hierarchical organisation. The *Article* pages contain information about the topics in the form of text, sound, graphics, video and animation. In addition, they include highlighted words linked to further information (*Pop-ups*). The *See Also* section at the bottom of the *Article* page contains topic-related links, whilst the sub-article icon contains special information about the topic. A bar at the bottom right of the screen leads to the next article on a topic and the arrow sign leads to the previous page, thus helping navigation through the encyclopaedia. The encyclopaedia provides different search tools for information seeking. These include the index search, containing an alphabetical list of key words, as well as the word search and animation search.

The students were introduced to the *Encyclopaedia of Science* a week before the actual study. After an introductory lesson on the software, the CD-ROM encyclopaedia was given to the students for further examination and exploration. Because of earlier experiences of using computers (including the use of CD-ROMs and the World Wide

Web) in school and home contexts, all the students in the classroom had been assessed as having adequate skills in the use of computers and multimedia. It must be noted, however, that the students were not given any special training for accessing and retrieving information with computer-based multimedia.

The learning situation

The learning content covered in the four sessions came from the students' current science curriculum and its major theme was 'Energy and its production'. The specific topics investigated in the sessions were: Energy and its forms, Electrical energy, Nuclear energy, and Electrical magnetism. The multimedia CD-ROM encyclopaedia covered these areas and its use was thought to create a flexible and interactive learning environment in which different information-seeking strategies and learning patterns could be used.

In the study, the students' task was to prepare a joint poster about the science topic they were exploring. Specifically, the students had 60 minutes to investigate, observe, discuss, and reflect on their understandings and representations of energy and its forms in the form of text, pictures, graphs, etc. on a joint poster. A joint poster task was selected so as to create inter-dependency between the students, hopefully leading to intensive collaboration and social meaning-making. Furthermore, the design of a poster in a multimedia-based small-group learning context was regarded as an enabling activity for the students to reflect and reconstruct their conceptual understanding on energy. The production of posters in small groups was a familiar learning activity in their classroom community. This learning activity was usually followed by a joint whole-class discussion in which each group presented their posters and reflected upon their investigation to the rest of the class.

The learning sessions began with oral instructions for the tasks. This included informing the students of the overall criteria by which the posters would be evaluated. It was emphasised that the information presented on the posters should be more than a reproduction of information from the multimedia encyclopaedia. More specific instructions concerning the poster task and the use of the CD-ROM encyclopaedia were also given to the students in written form. The teacher was available to the students in the classroom to support their learning activities. The teacher did not, however, intervene in the students' work unless requested to do so.

Approaches to investigation

The nature of the students' activity in this multimedia science context was investigated in four different sessions. The first and the fourth sessions were spent on individual work, whereas the second and the third sessions included pair work. The pairs remained the same in both these sessions. Pedagogically, the first session gave the students opportunities to practise and develop their individual working strategies with multimedia. It was felt that this would enrich the students' interaction and joint negotiation of their information-handling and processing strategies with multimedia while working in pairs. The final session of individual work gave the students opportunities to reflect upon their socially mediated working strategies and constructive activity. Although the empirical examples shown here are mostly derived from the pair situations, analyses of the individual working sessions have enriched data interpretation regarding the nature of students' sociocognitive and constructive activity in the multimedia context.

Both the individual and the pair sessions were video taped throughout and this recording was supplemented by the researchers' field notes. Three pairs were recorded at a time in the research classroom. During recording, the video cameras were placed so as to capture the students' use of the multimedia encyclopaedia, face-to-face interaction and the construction of the posters. This was possible because the video cameras were remote-controlled from the control room. After finishing the task, the students were asked to fill in a questionnaire that aimed at shedding light on their collaboration, task orientation and interpretation. In addition, stimulated recall interviews were held for each pupil individually after the first, second and fourth sessions. In the interview, the students were able to observe their own working processes on the video tapes. The interview questions were guided by the video tape and questionnaire data and their purpose was to increase understanding of the nature of students' sociocognitive activity and the development of conceptual understanding in the multimedia-based science learning context. The interviews were audio taped.

The analysis of the students' sociocognitive activity, as reflected in their social interaction followed the framework described in chapter 3 and involved a micro-analysis of the evolving peer interaction, by focusing on three analytic dimensions, namely the communicative functions of verbal interaction, cognitive processing and social processing. The first dimension of the analysis, the functional analysis, investigated the purpose and content of student talk in peer-group interaction.

It explored the communicative strategies used by participants in their social activity. The content analysis of the students' talk also revealed the nature of conceptual and procedural language that was constructed in students' moment-by-moment interactions in joint meaning-making. The second dimension, cognitive processing, focused on the ways in which students approached and processed learning tasks in their social activity. It aimed to highlight their working strategies and positions towards learning, knowledge and themselves as problem-solvers. The third dimension of the analysis, social processing, focused on the nature of the social relationships that were constructed in students' social activity. This included examining the types and forms of collaboration in peer groups. The latter two dimensions, cognitive and social processing, were investigated on an episode level, whereas the analysis of the communicative functions of peer interaction took the utterance as its unit of analysis. The three dimensions were treated separately for analytic purposes, although it was recognised that they were closely intertwined. In fact, the dimensions cannot be separated since each element gives meaning to all the others and simultaneously obtains meaning from them. An outline of the analysis framework is shown in table 2 in chapter 3.

The data on students' social interaction were illustrated with the help of analytical maps created for each peer group under investigation. The product of the analysis was, therefore, a series of situation-specific analytical maps that described the sequential evolution of peer-group interactions as they were constructed by students interacting with and acting on each other's messages. In addition to highlighting the dynamics of peer interaction, the maps showed the time dimension of the students' activity as well as some contextual information necessary for the interpretation of the social activity in question.

On-line video analysis served as a framework for creating analytical descriptions of the students' navigation and information-handling processes in the multimedia context. Other studies that have modelled students' navigation in multimedia have created visual representations of students' working via audit trails (Hill and Hannafin, 1997; Gay and Mazur, 1993). These studies, however, have mostly collected quantitative data for statistical comparisons. The present study, with its analytical descriptions, highlighted instead the situated processes of the students' navigation and information-handling activities when using a multimedia text.

The analysis of the students' conceptual understanding of the topic of energy was carried out by an evaluation of the quality of the posters the students designed as a part of their science investigation. The video

Table 9 Criteria for poster assessment

Points	Criteria
6	Clear, logical and illustrative work with demonstrations of interpretative thinking in a creative and consistent manner.
5	Logical and illustrative presentation with coherent structuring of information; may include a few pieces of copied text.
4	Some defects in the organisation and presentation of information, though fairly well illustrated and structured; contains some direct copying of information.
3	Demonstrates fairly poor structuring of information, with some of the students' own ideas and illustrations; includes a lot of copied text.
2	Fairly illogical presentation, including structural inconsistencies and no demonstration of own thinking; contains a high amount of direct copying.
1	Poorly illustrated and incoherent work with no demonstrations of interpretation of one's own.
0	Substantial deficiencies in all of the areas mentioned above.

analysis, as well as interview and questionnaire data, clarified and validated interpretations made on the basis of poster evaluations regarding the nature of the students' understandings and representations of different forms of energy and their production. The main foci in the evaluation of the posters were the logical structuring of knowledge, the demonstration of the students' own ideas and knowledge versus direct copying of text and clear and coherent illustration of information (see table 9).

Collaborative learning with multimedia

The results of the study will be discussed in two sections. Firstly, the process of the students' sociocognitive activity will be highlighted through descriptions of three cases in which we will try to characterise the nature of the students' social interaction, navigation processes and cognitive activity in the multimedia context. These examples will allow us to demonstrate the complex and dynamic nature of the students' working and learning processes in the multimedia-based learning context. Secondly, the results obtained from cross-analyses of all participants' work in the study will be summarised.

Case study 1: Elina and Jenni

Elina's and Jenni's sociocognitive activity in the learning situation turned out to be procedural and mechanical in nature, characterised by distinct working roles, product orientation, with an emphasis on appearance and length, and reproduction of multimedia-based science material. The girls' collaboration was mostly based on organising their working procedures rather than on critical selection, joint analysis of and reflection on the multimedia-based science material. Typically, one girl dictated text directly from the encyclopaedia and the other wrote down the dictated text onto the poster.

Detailed analyses of each session show that Elina's activity in the first individual session was less reproductive and more investigative in nature, whereas Jenni was already approaching the learning task in a product-oriented, surface-level manner. Interestingly, in her last individual working session, Elina seemed to adopt strategies from her experience in the pair sessions by focusing more on productivity and copying activity. The shift in the nature of Elina's working processes was also reflected in the quality of her posters, which scored 6 points in her first individual session but only 4 in her final session.

The functional analysis of Elina's and Jenni's oral interaction in the two pair-work sessions reveals that 26.4 per cent of the pair's verbal discourse was taken up with Organisational language functions. Other functions covering more than 10 per cent of the pair's discourse were the Interrogative (16.3 per cent), Affective (12.7 per cent) and Evaluative (10.1 per cent) functions. The evaluative activity was mostly directed to evaluating the appearance of the poster, and minor attention was paid to evaluating content-related materials or concepts, such as evaluating the selection and use of multimedia-based science material for the poster display.

The extract shown in table 10 is from Jenni's and Elina's second pair-work session. In this typical episode, Jenni and Elina discuss their working procedures by organising and planning their working roles and choosing material for their poster directly from the program. Although the girls investigate the multimedia-based science material, they seem not to reflect upon it but rather process it in a surface-level manner. This is also evidenced by the lack of conceptual language in the pair's discourse.

Elina and Jenni did not appear to have any difficulties with the technical use of the electronic encyclopaedia. However, their navigation in multimedia and hypertext was rather passive and linear in nature and it focused mainly on material presented on article pages and their links.

Their use of pop-ups, topic-related links and search tools was non-existent. The girls mainly concentrated on textual information in their task processing and little attention was given to material presented in the form of graphics, video clips and animations. Consequently, the girls' application of the CD-ROM encyclopaedia could be equated with the use of traditional, linear, narrative information sources, such as books.

The girls' information handling and processing strategies in their individual working sessions were rather similar. Both girls moved cautiously and systematically through the multimedia text. They seldom browsed through or navigated the material in a free-flow manner and did not visit many pages during their activity. Instead, they started their writing activity for the poster almost immediately.

The analysis of the quality of the posters that Elina and Jenni constructed shows that the information structure of the posters closely modelled the structure of the multimedia program they had worked with. Although the modelling activity resulted in illustrative and structured poster presentations, stimulated recall interviews suggested that the girls did not fully understand all the information they had presented in their posters. The girls reported having found the themes of the learning tasks difficult and felt that their lack of prior knowledge about energy had hindered their working processes and constructive activity.

Case study 2: Oliver and Anton

In addition to procedural information handling and task-division, Oliver's and Anton's processing of the learning task was found to include exploratory and strategic activity reflecting goal-orientation and attempts at interpretation. One of the distinct strategies applied by both these students in individual and pair-work sessions was the use of notes as support tools for the investigation of multimedia-based science material. The note-taking strategy seemed to assist the boys in conceptualising the topic under investigation and in structuring material for the poster. The pair's activity also indicated close collaboration in the organisation of working procedures and information handling in the multimedia. The actual processing of information from the multimedia program to the notes and then later to the poster appeared, however, to be mostly controlled by Oliver, who also took responsibility in navigation and dictation activity in the students' joint work.

The analysis of the students' verbal discourse in the two pair-work sessions shows that the language functions covering about 10 per

Table 10 An analytical map of peer interaction: the case of Elina and Jenni

Time	Participation		Transcribed peer interaction	Language functions	Cognitive processing	Social processing	Contextual notes
	145	Elina	I can write next	organises	procedural activity	collaboration in organising working procedures	
	146	Computer	'nuclear fusion occurs naturally in the sun . . .'				
	147	Jenni	yeah . . . there's the picture	informs	investigation of multimedia-based material		
	148	Computer	'inside the sun there is . . .'				
	149	Elina	it's exactly the one I'll draw here . . . it's going to be good when we draw . . .	informs, evaluates and organises			
	150	Jenni	or we could write down these	organises	planning		
00:20	151	Elina	you could then draw that one	organises	planning	collaboration in organising working procedures	

				a good example of surface level planning and rather disorganised approach to the learning theme
152	Jenni	you can write down these . . . and these	organises	
153	Elina	you mean these	checks by questioning	
154	Jenni	so this kind of a thing	checks by questioning	
155	Elina	yeah, you can do it	responds and encourages	procedural activity
156	Jenni	can I	requests affirmation	
157	Elina	well, draw then that one below	organises	
158	Jenni	well, I'll try that one	agrees	

cent or more of the students' discursive activity were the Organisational (25.7 per cent), Interrogative (14.7 per cent), Affective (12.9 per cent), Dictation (10.0 per cent) and Informative (9.8 per cent) functions. The high proportion of use of the Organisational function reflects the pair's procedural activity while working on the task, while their use of the Interrogative and Informative functions gives evidence of joint meaning-making. The significant presence of the Affective function in the pair's verbal discourse can be explained by the students' playful activities while investigating animations and demos in the multimedia. A closer analysis of the use of the Dictation function illustrates task-division between the students and demonstrates that Oliver engaged in dictation activity much more often than Anton (56 instances versus 11).

Anton and Oliver were found to be significantly more active in browsing the multimedia material than the students described in case 1. Although the boys seemed not to navigate the pop-ups, they carefully went through all subject-related article pages and utilised related links. The students were also found to concentrate on pictures, animations and sounds. Although they partly used these facilities for entertainment purposes, some pictures and animations enhanced reflective joint discussions about the phenomena studied.

The interaction episode shown in table 11 is taken from the second pair-work session, during which Oliver and Anton were investigating nuclear energy and its production process. The boys showed a good deal of enthusiasm towards multimedia animations. It is noteworthy that in this extract they were reasoning and explaining the phenomena presented in the animation to each other. They also showed concern about the topic of their science investigation, which seemed to support their joint meaning-making.

An investigation of the students' information-handling and processing activity across the four sessions shows that Oliver's working strategies were somewhat more goal oriented and structured in nature than those of Anton. Oliver was also seen to be a more active navigator who tried to utilise and comprehend topic-related science material from the multimedia program in a strategic manner.

The analysis of the quality of posters the students constructed during their individual and pair-work sessions shows somewhat unexpected results. Whereas Oliver designed a very coherent, informative and logical poster presentation in his first individual session, the works produced in the pair-work sessions and in Anton's individual sessions were rather ill-structured, with very little text, and contained conceptually incoherent sentences. However, in neither of the sessions had the boys copied material directly from the multimedia; rather they had aimed at their own interpretation and representation. This finding raises important questions in relation to the evaluation of students' learning, and to the design of learning situations. When it comes to the evaluation of students' learning, it seems that the mere assessment of students' products does not give a full picture of students' learning, but that it is also important to take account of the nature of the students' working and learning processes in the actual learning situation. In fact, process-analyses may guide the construction of evaluation criteria for assessing learning outcomes.

Case study 3: Laurie and Thomas

The analyses of Laurie's and Thomas' working processes in the learning situation reveal an interplay between procedural, product-oriented activity and exploratory, reflective activity. This may partly be explained by the students' different working strategies and orientations, as demonstrated at the outset in the first individual working sessions. Whereas Thomas appeared to invest time in interpreting material and learning through strategic working processes, such as constructing notes, Laurie's individual work relied on copying material from the multimedia text, particularly the presentation structure. A further analysis of the nature of the students' sociocognitive activity across the pair sessions indicated, however, that gradually Thomas followed Laurie's working strategies and the boys began to copy more material from the software instead of investing time in joint interpretative activity. The reason for the increase in the pair's copying activity appeared, from their stimulated recall interviews, to result from their weak conceptual understanding of nuclear energy.

Although the students' pair-work activity reflected their collaboration in joint meaning-making and in the organisation of working processes and information handling, there were distinct working roles for each student. In many instances, Thomas dictated material to Laurie, and Laurie, in his turn, wrote down the selected material as notes and onto the poster. The functional analysis of the students' verbal discourse in the two pair-work sessions shows that the Organisational (22.2 per cent), Interrogative (15.5 per cent), Responsive (14.1 per cent) and Dictation (8.9 per cent) language functions were typical communicative strategies employed by this pair. These functions, except for Dictation, were rather equally distributed between the students, indicating shared working processes in the learning situation.

Table 11 An analytical map of peer interaction: the case of Oliver and Anton

Time		Participation	Transcribed peer interaction	Language functions	Cognitive processing	Social processing	Contextual notes
00:05:00	50	Computer	(demos on explosions)		exploratory activity	collaboration and joint investigation	
	51	Anton	that's a cool explosion	evaluates			
	52	Computer	(demo is finishing)				
	53	Anton	so those explosions produce energy	reasons	explaining the phenomena		
	54	Computer	'chain reactions'				
	55	Oliver	look . . . like this then	organises	directing attention		
	56	Anton	how cool . . . how cool . . . put it on	evaluates, organises	investigating		
	57	Oliver	I cannot do that	informs			The program does not allow it since it is not a demo
	58	Anton	oh . . . what a shame . . . it could've been cool I can write, I can write	affectional expression, organises	procedural activity	collaboration in organising working procedures	
	59	Computer	'nuclear physics'				

60	Anton	let's put something	organises			
61	Computer	nuclear physics . . . nuclear . . . nuc . . .				plays with the software
62	Anton	what was our topic after all	requests information	content-related discussion	joint meaning making	
63	Oliver	oh gee . . . could it	replies in an affective mood			
64	Anton	nuclear energy	informs			
65	Oliver	and its production	informs			
66	Computer	'in the sun . . .'				demo on the sun
67	Oliver	we'd rewind it	organises	procedural activity	collaboration in infomation handling	refers to the video-clip
68	Anton	hey hey let's take it	organises			
69	Oliver	this	requests affirmation			
70	Anton	yeah put it on	replies and organises			
71	Computer	. . . 'several nuclear reactions take place in the sun every second'				
72	Oliver	several nuclear reactions take place in the sun every second	repeats			

The extract shown in table 12 is derived from Laurie's and Thomas' third pair-work session, during which the students were working on a topic dealing with nuclear energy. This episode was characterised by collaboration and joint meaning-making, including joint planning, raising questions, and investigation of the multimedia-based science material. The latter part of the extract showed a rather exceptional tutoring episode during which Thomas argued and explained his views to Laurie on the hierarchical structure of the concepts related to nuclear energy and how they should be presented in the poster display.

Both Laurie and Thomas were seen to be experienced users of multimedia. The students were observed throughout the sessions to be actively involved in browsing multiple pages and using program search facilities. They also showed interest in animations.

The evaluation of the posters these students constructed as a part of their science investigation shows that these were logical and illustrative and followed a coherent information structure. In particular, the second pair-work session resulted in a poster that reflected interpretative thinking and creativity. Thomas' low poster score from his last individual working session was explained by him as resulting partly from his tiredness and lack of relevant conceptual knowledge. Also noteworthy is the fact that the students' high reliance on the information structure presented in the multimedia led to structured and coherent poster presentations, despite the fact that they did not necessarily understand all the relationships and connections between different science concepts.

Cross-analyses of the whole data

The cross-analyses of the whole data sample reveal that the students' activity was mostly confined to management and organisation of working processes and to procedural handling of the multimedia-based science material. The nature of their verbal discourse appeared to be composed of sequences indicating quite procedural, surface-level activity. From the point of view of communicative functions, typical discourse episodes consisted of Organisational, Dictation, Judgemental, Repetition and Affective functions. Social interaction more typical of critical examination and exploratory activity, such as reasoning, arguing, speculating and evaluating, was much rarer. At a conceptual level of analysis, social interaction focusing on interpretative and reflective investigation of energy and its forms was infrequent.

The data analysis suggests the presence of different strategies for information handling and processing when working with multimedia.

Whereas passive navigators visited only a few pages and followed topic links as suggested by the main folder, it was more typical of active navigators to visit many pages, navigate in page-related links and use index searches. Active navigators also showed more interest than passive navigators in animations, demos and other program facilities. The general observation was, however, that these students' navigation and search strategies in processing multimedia-based science material were not very effective. Those students who actively used various searches while handling multimedia-based science material were not very successful in processing that information so as to construct an understanding of the science involved. This was also reflected in the students' posters, analysis of which indicates that – with few exceptions – there were no marked differences in the quality of the posters produced by active and passive navigators.

Another finding concerning the students' information handling and processing in multimedia is that although the students used multiple forms of media during task processing, they relied heavily on textual information in their final posters. Other forms of media were found to have a more entertaining rather than educational role in the students' problem-solving activity. This became clearly evident when analysing the nature of the students' verbal discourse while examining non-textual media. Instead of having topic-related discussions, the students' discourse tended to be playful and directed to surface-level or off-task activities. The non-linear presentation of information also seemed to cause difficulties for some of the students in processing multimedia-based science material into a linear form, giving rise to structural and conceptual difficulties in the construction of posters.

The data also reveal slight variation in the students' working strategies, particularly in relation to note taking whilst processing the poster task. Whereas most of the students copied information from the encyclopaedia directly onto notes and/or posters, there were some students who used notes as an interpretative strategy for their science investigation and construction of poster presentations. Yet, the students' working strategies as a whole seemed not to include active information processing, such as comparing, critical evaluation or combining their own experiences or knowledge with the information encountered within the program.

The analysis of the nature of the students' collaboration in dyadic conditions exposes distinct working roles, despite the fact that the students were working jointly on the same task towards a common goal. In most cases, the students' collaboration consisted of joint activity, during which one of the students was responsible for navigation

Table 12 An analytical map of peer interaction: the case of Laurie and Thomas

Time	Participation		Transcribed peer interaction	Language functions	Cognitive processing	Social processing	Contextual notes
00:08	83	Laurie	hey . . . we must see . . . hey . . . how one produces energy	organises	planning	collaboration and joint meaning-making	
	84	Thomas	be quiet	affective utterance			
	85	Computer	' . . . '				
	86	Laurie	well . . how do you produce it . . .	requests information	raising questions		
	87	Thomas	what	requests information			
	88	Laurie	nuclear energy . . . nuclear ener . . .	replies and provides information			
	89	Thomas	production of nuclear energy	informs			
	90	Laurie	where is it	requests information	investigation		
00:09	91	Computer	'nuclear energy'		exploratory activity	collaboration	
	92	Thomas	here . . . uran . . . 235 . . . here it is . . . I see	informs and explains			
	93	Computer	'fission reactors'				

Investigating related topics from the multimedia software

	94	Thomas	okay . . . shall we write about this	organises and asks for affirmation	planning	
	95	Laurie	I don't know	replies		
00.10	106	Thomas	don't write it in the centre	organises	designing	joint negotiation
	107	Laurie	nuclear ener . . . why not	reads aloud, disagrees		
	108	Thomas	well . . . you see . . . nuclear energy and its production is a larger topic and these are sub-topics . . . nuclear energy and its production . . . that sub-title comes here	argues and organises	arguing, explaining	tutoring
	109	Laurie	it isn't the sub-title for this	argues		
	110	Thomas	no no but it's the sub-title for this and this is the sub-title for this so this is the sub-title for this and this is the same as this	argues		
	111	Laurie	yeah but it doesn't have to be in that corner	argues		
00:11	112	Thomas	yes it does if that is then . . . it's logical . . . otherwise somebody may think that's something new	argues	arguing, explaining	
	113	Laurie	heheh . . . give me the rubber . . . okay then . . .	organises, agrees		

and dictated text to the other student, who was responsible for writing down poster text and other material. In this study, collaborative small-group work seemed to increase the students' procedural and organisational activity, instead of strengthening the joint construction of reasoned selection, interpretation and evaluation of multimedia-based science material.

In summary, the students' sociocognitive activity can be characterised as product oriented with little evidence of exploratory activity relevant for knowledge construction. Interaction episodes typical of meaningful learning, such as thinking aloud, commenting on observations, questioning, social construction of information, evaluation and connecting new information to pre-existing knowledge, were infrequent in the data. The nature of the students' sociocognitive activity was also reflected in the quality of the posters, showing in many cases direct copying of text from the encyclopaedia and incoherent conceptual representations.

Discussion and conclusions

The results of this study shed some light on some important features that need to be considered in technology-based learning. On the one hand, these features are technology-specific and are related to the handling and processing of multimedia-based learning material. On the other hand, they concern broader questions of learning and instruction, such as the design and evaluation of technology-based learning environments. As the following discussion will show, these features are closely intertwined and, consequently, need to be examined in parallel.

Central components regulating learning processes have been identified in the subject-related knowledge base and in the cognitive and metacognitive strategies learners use in their learning activity (Pressley and McCormick, 1995; Vosniadou, 1996; Young, 1997). As evidenced by the present study and some others, constructive activity in multimedia-based learning, which includes active structuring and organisation activity, appears to require the use of diverse cognitive strategies related to navigation, hypertext processing and more general learning skills (Goldman, 1997; Hill and Hannafin, 1997). From the results of this study, these manifold strategies are socially and situationally defined and dynamically constructed in evolving interactions within a social context. In addition, the application of particular strategies seems to be mediated by the students' conceptions of the learning situation and its requirements as well as by their prior domain knowledge and earlier experiences of processing and handling multimedia-based science material.

In this study, analyses of the students' information-seeking and navigation processes while using the CD-ROM encyclopaedia revealed activity patterns more typical of novice users of multimedia. In many cases, the students approached and handled multimedia-based material in a rather structured and linear manner with little use of the available search tools. In addition, they appeared to let the multimedia program and its information structures guide their navigation and information-processing activity, which mostly focused on material presented in a hypertext format. Although conceptually and semantically coherent multimedia-based material can implicitly guide students' information handling and processing towards desired learning, this may not be the case with all kinds of multimedia material used for educational purposes. In general, the students seemed not to consider the fact that when information is presented in a network-like structure, the reader has to be even more active and strategic in order to create coherent representations of the topic under investigation (Foltz, 1996).

Although learners' navigation and information-handling skills in multimedia are likely to be linked with the nature of their constructive activity, insufficient prior domain knowledge also appears to constrain learners' strategic activity and information processing of multimedia-based material (Goldman, 1997). The results of this study confirm this by indicating that the students had rather weak conceptual understanding of energy and its forms. Other studies of the reading process have reported that readers with greater subject matter knowledge find it easier to distinguish important from less important information and that they are less seduced by interesting but unimportant details. In addition, students with high domain knowledge have a tendency to concentrate on constructing relationships among ideas presented in the text (Garner *et al.*, 1991). Such constructive activities were scarcely present in the students observed in the present study.

Learners' conceptions of knowledge and learning, as well as their expectations based on earlier experiences of similar tasks and their goals, play an important role in defining the nature of constructive activity in a learning situation. These features also regulate the nature of the learning resulting from a particular activity (Baker and Brown, 1984). In the present study, the posters that the students constructed were found to consist mainly of information that closely modelled and represented the content and structure of the actual CD-ROM encyclopaedia. Furthermore, the nature of the students' sociocognitive activity was observed to be procedural and product oriented in nature.

On the basis of these findings, it appears that the students' conceptions of the task goals and of effective learning activity patterns contrasted with those of the instructional setting.

For the purposes of this research, the poster task was chosen for a number of reasons. Contemporary conceptions of learning emphasise the need for challenging, complex and open-ended tasks that are based on student inquiries and the social construction of knowledge (McGilly, 1994). The instructional goal of the learning situation was that the students, both individually and in pairs, would investigate, evaluate and discuss the science topic with the help of a multimedia CD-ROM and reflect their own representations and understandings of the domain in posters. This learning activity was expected to provide the students with opportunities to plan and organise their own research and problem solving by selecting, assessing and synthesising information from multiple sources both individually and in a socially shared learning activity. On the basis of the study, the intended goals of the instructional setting were clearly not achieved in most of the student cases investigated. In fact, it appears that the learning task was conceptualised by the students as an activity that required procedural working and re-presenting material rather than investigating and critiquing it. What makes these results alarming is the fact that the pedagogical setting and the task described here reflect a rather common educational practice often used for small-group work activities in more traditional and technology-based learning situations.

Other studies have also reported students to be adaptive to their instructional settings (Goldman, 1996). Task demands, cultural norms and ground rules of the classroom community regulate students' working and learning strategies and continuously shape their conceptions of what counts as learning and knowledge under certain circumstances. Consequently, the mere uptake of technology and the design of new instructional settings with modified learning goals are unlikely to make radical changes in students' constructive activity unless serious attention is also paid to the learning culture of the classroom in question.

Pedagogical considerations of multimedia-based instruction

Although technology has great potential to support learning, it is important to recognise that technology-based learning has its own characteristics that need to be taken into consideration when designing and applying technology to the practices of learning and instruction

(Salomon, 1997). Standard applications, such as CD-ROM encyclo-paedias, do not include any built-in pedagogical supports, and, usually, pedagogical principles were not central in their design. This increases the need to pay careful attention to the design of the instructional settings and learning activities in which multimedia is embedded. This includes some consideration of the nature of the support students need in handling and processing multimedia-based learning material (Goldman, 1996; Lawless and Brown, 1997).

The results of the present study demonstrate that students are likely to need support for strategic activity in multimedia-based learning. What seems to be important, on the basis of earlier research, is that pedagogical supports should be embedded in the learning situation and the tools used, and that the strategies and skills they are intended to foster are introduced during learners' self-initiated activity rather than by direct teaching (Young, 1997). In the following section, three interconnected dimensions of multimedia-based instruction will be considered, with special emphasis on necessary pedagogical supports.

Supporting learning through careful instructional design

In order to ensure active knowledge construction in multimedia-based learning environments, it is important that close attention be directed to the design of the learning situations in which multimedia is embedded. It seems important that the learning tasks be adjusted in accordance with students' abilities, domain knowledge and interests. Moreover, learning tasks need to be challenging, authentic and meaningful, and to take careful account of the potential of technology in supporting the intended learning goals. For example, in the present study, the use of multimedia authoring software could have been considered as a tool for students to show their understanding of the science domain they were investigating in the CD-ROM encyclopaedia, instead of a poster task. As evidenced by other studies (e.g. Jonassen, Beissner and Yacci, 1993), software programs that allow the construction of concept maps, graphic organisers, causal interaction maps or structural maps can be useful and effective means for representing relationships among concepts. In addition to careful instructional design, it seems as important to pay attention to the established learning culture of the students. For effective learning, it is essential that the students' goals, values and appreciated activity patterns coincide with those embedded in the learning situation.

Supporting collaborative peer-group learning

Besides different instructional arrangements, such as peer tutoring and jigsaw-methods, which encourage inter-dependency between learners working in pairs or small groups (see e.g. Cohen, 1994), it seems important that, for the joint construction of conceptual knowledge, attention be paid to encouraging students' explanation generation and joint reasoning in multimedia-based environments. This can be achieved by creating student-sensitive, contextualised supports for collaborative meaning-making in the actual learning situation as well as by careful teacher interventions, for example in the form of reciprocal teaching (Fisher, 1993; Palincsar and Brown, 1984; Rosenshine and Meister, 1994). In addition, attention has to be directed to students' collaborative learning skills and communication skills as constructed by their classroom learning culture.

Supporting information handling and processing of multimedia-based material

Effective information handling and processing of multimedia-based material requires multiple skills, some of which are technology specific and some of which involve more general information-handling and learning skills. Skills connected to the use of multimedia involve the capacity to deal with multiple sources of information presented in a networked structure. Multimedia-based information structures and their specific discourses are often strange to novice users; consequently, for effective learning, students need the experiences and necessary skills to handle and process multimedia-based material. Otherwise, learning with multimedia applications can easily turn into knowledge transmission via technological aids instead of constructive and socially mediated learning.

While the use of multimedia enables learner control, information processing within multimedia environments may be particularly difficult for learners limited in both domain knowledge and cognitive skills. Students who do not possess the prerequisite amount of conceptual knowledge, cognitive skills and multimedia experiences may easily get lost in the environment and be unable to comprehend the information presented, or to identify what information is needed or where to locate it (Charney, 1987). While the ability to control one's learning activity can promote learning and strengthen interest and motivation, unrestricted control, lack of learning skills and misinterpretations of learning goals can dampen the power of learning in such an environment. Consequently, the instructional design of multimedia-based learning should consider the scope and nature of learner control appropriate for particular students, learning tasks and classroom cultures.

The design, realisation and evaluation of multimedia-based instruction following the above guidelines is an exciting and highly acute challenge for researchers, educators and software designers. If we are to make the most of the potential multimedia can offer for learning and to provide students with adequate technological and social skills required in the current and future society, this challenge needs to be tackled in the near future.

Part III

Classroom interaction and learning

Implications for classroom practice

9 Learning from the research

The implications of classroom interaction studies

In this book we have outlined the rationale for investigating students' classroom interactions. This rationale is greatly influenced by theoretical views that emphasise the social nature of learning. In these views, social interaction and language are seen as highly significant tools for communication and learning (Vygotsky, 1962, 1978). Our interests in classroom interactions from the viewpoint of students have also been pedagogically inspired, in that we have been intrigued by the diverse roles, operations, and meanings of students' social interactions in today's classrooms. Particularly, the increasing use of student-centred learning situations, characterised by open-ended tasks and collaborative working modes, seems to have modified the traditional interaction patterns in classrooms and changed the roles of the teacher and students as communicators and learners. Moreover, the application of diverse tools of information and communication technology have also influenced classroom learning practices and interactions, giving students new opportunities and challenges for learning. All these changes in contemporary classrooms have urged educators to rethink their pedagogical practices and evaluation methods. As highlighted by the case studies discussed in part two of this book, we believe that a micro-level investigation of the dynamics of students' classroom interactions can reveal important information about the enabling conditions for productive interaction and learning in modern classrooms.

How do students interact during collaborative group work?

One of the principal motivations for beginning the programme of research described in this book was dissatisfaction with currently available ways of thinking about the uses of talk amongst students engaged in collaborative learning. As we argued earlier, peer interaction has increased in many classrooms as the result of new conceptions of learning. It has, consequently, become very important for teachers and researchers to understand better how meanings and knowledge are constructed between students while working in small groups on various learning activities. Since the ground-breaking work of Barnes and Todd (1977), a number of approaches have been suggested for examining group interaction during learning episodes, particularly the talk used during these interactions. A significant insight deriving from our own work in this area has been the development of a functional analysis of such talk. This analysis takes us beyond the simple classification of types of talk to a much richer and context-specific way of describing and discussing student-to-student talk. The Functional Analysis of Children's Classroom Talk (FACCT) system allows both teachers and researchers to enhance their awareness of patterns of talk in classroom social learning and to give due attention to the contextual influences on the talk produced.

Because this system is context specific in its analysis, it is impossible to present it now as a fixed analysis system. It has, however, proved a useful tool in extending the observation powers of teachers as they try to maximise the learning of their students, and for that reason we present it again here in table 13. This version of the FACCT system has been developed from that presented in chapter 4 by the addition of a number of sub-functions that have proved useful in allowing a closer-grained look at talk.

It should also be borne in mind that talk is not all there is to student interaction. As we argued in chapter 3, there are other dimensions, such as cognitive and social processing, to be taken into account.

The richness of students' social interaction in student-centred classrooms

The case studies discussed earlier all highlight the diversity and richness of students' social interaction in classrooms where student-centred learning methods and practices are encouraged. In each study, the nature of the students' social interaction indicates that in student-centred learning situations the learners are given more opportunities to be active members of the classroom, shaping the content and form of communication. The purposes for which the students use their oral language across the case studies highlight the diverse communicative strategies that students use for making meaning in collaboration with other members of their classrooms. The natures of these communicative strategies also illuminate the students' active role in the

Table 13 The Functional Analysis of Children's Classroom Talk (FACCT) System

Language function	Description
Informative *Sub-functions*	Providing information *Information derived from knowledge/ideas* *Information derived from resources* *Situational information*
Interrogative *Sub-functions*	Asking questions *Questions requiring information* *Questions requiring social approval or acceptance*
Organisational	Organising behaviour
Judgemental	Expressing agreement or disagreement
Affective	Expression of personal feelings
Compositional *Sub-functions*	Producing writing *Creating writing* *Revising writing* *Dictating writing*
Responsive	Answering questions
Reproductional *Sub-functions*	Reproducing spoken or written language *Reading aloud* *Repeating verbal formulations*
External Thinking	Thinking aloud in accompaniment of a task
Expositional	Oral language accompanying the demonstration of a phenomena
Argumentational	Reasoning in oral language
Imaginative	Introducing or expressing imaginative situations
Experiential	Expressing personal experiences
Heuristic	Expressing discovery
Hypothetical	Putting forward a hypothesis
Intentional	Signalling intention to participate in discourse

construction of their own knowledge. In addition to the cognitive benefits of engaging in classroom interaction, interaction and oral language seemed to serve a social function. Consequently, when engaging in classroom interactions the students were found to be not only elaborating their current understandings about the domain in question but also learning to participate in social activity with others.

The study discussed in chapter 4, which compared the interaction in teacher-centred and student-centred classrooms, effectively highlighted the differences in the quality and quantity of students' oral language across these two styles of classroom organisation. The range of language functions found in student-centred classrooms included giving information, making judgements, organising work or action, arguing, composing, thinking aloud, expressing emotions and imagining. The use of language for all these purposes suggests that the students had taken upon themselves a powerful role in meaning-making, both in cognitive and social terms. In teacher-centred classrooms, on the other hand, the role of the student as a participant in classroom interaction was found to be quite different. Here, the students were found to engage more in the role of the respondent in providing specific pieces of information to the teaching–learning process already determined by the teacher. The active role of the teacher as a determiner of the classroom interaction was also seen in the students' use of the intentional function when asking permission to take part in conversation. The ways in which other functions, such as Reproductional, Interrogative and Judgemental, were used in students' oral language provide an indication of students' heavy dependence on their teachers for the interactional context for learning in these classrooms.

The case studies discussed in chapters 5 to 8 give further evidence of the existence of rich and diverse classroom interaction among students when working on peer-centred small-group tasks. These studies not only highlight the possible cognitive and social gains and achievements resulting in and from such vivid interactions, but also make obvious the challenges posed by the student-centred classroom, in terms of organisation.

The study exploring the nature of students' oral language interactions during a collaborative writing experience at the computer also demonstrates the potential of the social context created by the use of word processors to engage students in social construction of writing and learning. In this study, the students were found to take an active role in sharing and constructing their understandings when communicating their ideas and thinking about the possible contents and forms of writing with a peer. The students' verbal interactions in the word processing context included giving information, composing, questioning, making judgements, organising activities, external thinking, responding to peers questions, repeating peers' expressions and concepts, and expressing emotions. What was also noteworthy in these findings was that the students did not often seem to engage in

exploratory talk or participate in argumentative discourse when creating their joint text. From the point of view of the students' literacy
learning, this was perhaps slightly worrying, and consideration might
be paid to how to support such interaction in the course of the collaborative process in the future.

The case study discussed in chapter 6 focused on the nature of
children's talk in an early years classroom with a specific emphasis
on questions of leadership and control. This study also involved
children working in collaborative small groups. The social interaction
of the classroom was studied in terms of its communicative functions
when investigating the nature of the children's verbal interactions
when engaged on science and mathematics tasks. In the study, the
children's personal profiles and their reflection on their interaction
was also taken into account. The findings of this study illuminate the
ways in which the nature of the children's social interaction is shaped
by the nature of the learning tasks. This was seen in terms of both
the quality and quantity of the children's classroom interactions. For
example, the occurrence and nature of the External Thinking function,
argumentative uses of language, Judgemental function, giving information, posing questions and repeating the peer's utterances seemed to
vary across the tasks, giving evidence of the existence of the diverse
skills students possessed when taking part in social learning.

This study also identified the uses of oral language that appeared to
be associated with styles of leadership within the groups of children.
In the study, the children who predominantly adopted a leadership
role within the group were found to judge each other's comments or
activities, take the role in organising activities and working processes
as well as engage in argumentation. These uses of language appeared
in some cases to result in dominative activity, giving rise to unequal participation in students' interaction and meaning-making. The students'
social skills and personality characteristics appeared to play a role in
directing the interaction into a collaborative mode.

The case study in chapter 7 investigated the nature of students' social
interaction when working in pairs on an open design task in geometry.
Here, specific attention was paid to the students' social and cognitive
processes evident in small-group interaction when working on a less
structured mathematics learning task. In this study, the analysis of
students' social interaction was extended from a functional analysis
of students' oral language to the investigation of the dynamics of
peer interaction from cognitive and social viewpoints. The construction
of analytical maps characterising the moment-by-moment evolution of
students' interactions within pairs helped to unravel the elements in the

students' interactions that appeared to support and challenge collaborative interaction and reasoning. In addition, the analytical maps highlighted the nature of the students' interaction and gave evidence of the potential of open-ended small-group activities to generate active reasoning and exploratory student talk. The study also illustrated some of the challenges that open-ended tasks may pose for students, leading to the rise of asymmetric, non-productive interactions. In the study, symmetric interaction was characterised by equal participation in social interaction, including joint reasoning of problem-solving strategies and active conceptualisation and visualisation of the situation. Asymmetric interaction was evidenced by incoherent social interaction, in which divergent strategies and verbal conceptualisations were used without constructing a shared meaning. Furthermore, the problem-solving activity appeared to rest on mainly disintegrated strategies, which focused on local measuring and constructing activities with little global vision. These findings suggest the need for close monitoring of students' social activity in group problem solving in order to ensure productive, task-focused interaction and learning.

The final case study in this set (chapter 8) investigated the students' social interaction and cognitive activity when handling and processing information in a multimedia-based science learning task. The prime goal in this study was to highlight the social context of science learning when student pairs worked on a poster task and used multimedia CD-ROM encyclopaedias as their information sources. The students' working processes were also investigated during periods of individual activity in order to shed more light on the social effects of processing multimedia-based information in small groups. In the study, the students' end products were also evaluated in order to investigate any links between quality of outcome and the nature of students' social interaction and cognitive activity. The findings of the study indicate that the students' social interaction was focused mostly on managing and organising working processes and on the procedural handling of information from the CD-ROM. In most cases, the students' verbal interaction was found to be composed of Organisational, Dictation, Judgemental, Repetition and Affective functions of language. All this indicates procedural, surface-level activity in which the students' goal was to produce neat poster displays instead of critically concentrating on thoughtful investigation of the science material represented in the multimedia program. The students' executive activity was also evidenced in the quality of their poster displays, of which analysis revealed that they had quite often directly copied text from the encyclopaedia, leading to incoherent conceptual representations.

The analysis of the nature of the students' collaboration within pairs exposed distinct working roles between the students, with one student often being responsible for navigation and dictation and the other for writing down poster text and material. A comparison of the students' individual and pair work suggests, in fact, that in social conditions their procedural and executive activity actually increased. These findings suggest a need for close attention to be paid to pedagogical practices when applying social working modes and new technology in teaching and learning.

Maximising the potential of students' classroom interaction

The research studies discussed in this book, taken in conjunction with those reported in recent years by other researchers, provide convincing evidence of the positive effects of peer-group interaction on students' cognitive, social and affective development across domains (Azmitia, 1996; Cohen, 1994; Forman and Cazden, 1985; Sharan, Shachar and Levine, 1999; Stevens and Slavin, 1995). The diversity of learners' prior knowledge and experience seems to provide a large resource base for a group's knowledge construction, giving opportunities for self-reflection and joint reasoning (Teasley, 1995). Nevertheless, although peer-group activity can offer students extended opportunities for active participation in social interaction, not all kinds of interactions lead to joint reasoning and knowledge construction. The quality of learning in peer groups is strongly associated with the nature of the inter-actions and the collaboration in which learners engage while working on academic tasks (King, 1992; Peterson *et al.*, 1984; Webb, 1991; Webb, Troper and Fall, 1995). Furthermore, the roles of the instruc-tional setting and its task-specific features in shaping the nature of social interaction in peer groups have been widely recognised (Cohen, 1994; Fuchs *et al.*, 2000; Sharan, Shacher and Levine, 1999).

Studies of the behaviours that promote learning in peer interactive groups have suggested that the construction of explanations that are procedurally clear and conceptually rich can support social knowledge construction (Fuchs *et al.*, 1996; Webb, Troper and Fall, 1995). Other forms of interaction conducive to social learning have included asking appropriate questions (King, 1989), exchanging ideas, justifications, speculations, inferences, hypotheses and conclusions (Cohen, 1994). Research grounded in sociocognitive theories has shown that engag-ing in and resolving conflicts with peers also encourages learning (Doise and Mugny, 1984; Nastasi, Clements and Battista, 1990). In resolving disagreements, learners explain, justify or question positions and approaches. They seek new information, or adopt alternative points of view and conceptualisations (Perret-Clermont, Perret and Bell, 1991). Socioculturally oriented studies of peer-group interaction and learning have also increased understanding of the ways in which particular interaction patterns such as *exploratory talk*, in which participants operate and build on each other's reasoning via verbal language and other semiotic tools, give learners opportunities for joint reasoning and co-construction of common knowledge (Edwards and Mercer, 1987; Fisher, 1996; Mercer, 1996).

Peer-group interaction and learning is a widely studied topic. There is, however, still little evidence concerning the dynamics of students' social interactions and oral language during productive group learning sessions, particularly in less structured small-group learning situations, such as those described in this book (Champagne, 1992; Hogan, Nastasi and Pressley, 2000). The goal in the case studies discussed here has been to generate new insights into classroom interaction in student-centred learning situations. This has been attempted through multi-level analyses of students' classroom interactions as captured through a range of data collection methods and procedures. It is hoped that the insights generated by these studies might lead to improvements in classroom practice, both in terms of implementing and supporting small-group learning as well as in creating effective and meaningful learning situations.

The learning situations in which the students worked in the case studies discussed here were mostly designed for collaborative small-group activities and consisted of open-ended tasks. These tasks could be approached from different perspectives with diverse strategies. In the tasks, it was usually the students who initiated and posed the problems and started to investigate and solve them. The openness of the learning situation was usually also reflected in the students' end products, which were often unique to each student group. An important element in the learning situations was also the possibility of communicating ideas and thinking through versatile tools. Although the students' oral language functioned as an important tool for communicating and meaning-making, in some of the case studies other tools, such as computers, objects, images and laboratory tools, seemed to work as mediators of meaning, assisting the students' sharing of their perspectives and conceptualisations. A number of features, therefore, seemed to support students' active participation in social interaction and meaning-making. These could be listed as:

- a complex and open learning situation;
- students initiating meaning-making;
- opportunities to approach and conceptualise the task with different problem-solving strategies;
- opportunities to use a range of semiotic tools, including informal and formal language.

The open nature of the learning situation was found to pose challenges for students' social interaction and collective problem-solving. This could clearly be seen in the case studies discussed in this book, particularly in those in which the interplay between social and cognitive elements in social interaction was investigated. Analyses of the students' social interaction revealed differences in the nature of their collaborative relationships across the groups. Symmetric interaction, including task-based argumentation and tutoring, seemed to support collaborative interaction, whereas dominative and socially competitive interaction seemed to hinder this. In groups where there were repeated cognitive and social conflicts, the outcome was in some cases asymmetric interaction and problem solving, thus diminishing the potential for collaborative interaction. In some cases, however, conflict situations resulted in peer tutoring episodes or argumentative episodes, during which one member of the group scaffolded others towards a joint understanding. These findings indicate the importance of students' social and cognitive skills in maintaining productive, task-focused interaction.

In the case studies, collaborative interaction seemed to be characterised by equal participation in social interaction, including joint reasoning and use of problem-solving strategies and active conceptualisation of the situation. Collaborative interaction seemed to be supported by reciprocal attempts to create a joint meaning when making problem solving visible via explanation and demonstration. The students' appreciation of each other's contribution to problem solving and their explicit communication of this to their partner(s) was also found to support social interaction and to promote their sense of being legitimate participants in a collaborative endeavour. Interactions that appeared to support collaborative problem-solving were those that helped develop the reasoning of other group members. Symmetric interaction was also seen in contributions that paraphrased a partner's reasoning as well as in exchanges where ideas and suggestions were challenged (see also Azmitia and Montgomery, 1993; Berkowitz, Oser and Althof, 1987; Kruger, 1993; Tolmie *et al.*, 1993). Yet, in order to establish and maintain a shared focus in conflict situations, it was also important that group members stayed in a task-focused mode and kept their personal views in check.

In summary, the case studies discussed in this book demonstrate that the social and cognitive processes inherent in peer problem-solving are highly dynamic in nature, shaping students' social interactions on a moment-by-moment basis. Vion (1992), when characterising the dynamic nature of interaction situations, introduces the concept of *heterogeneous interactive space* (cf. Grossen, 1994). This refers to the social, cognitive and interactive roles and contexts that interactors have to negotiate in order to achieve a joint understanding. When investigating peer interaction and the conditions that shape its nature, it seems important to recognise that the processes and outcomes of such interaction are embedded within the larger context of peer relationships as well as in societal and institutional norms (Sharan, Shachar and Levine, 1999; Tharp and Gallimore, 1988). Consequently, besides the importance of investigating the complexities of the situated dynamics of interpersonal interactions in learning situations, it might be useful in the future to explore broader cultural influences shaping and modifying the processes and outcomes of peer interaction.

The role of the teacher

In this book, the focus has been on classroom interaction from the viewpoint of the students. We have paid little explicit attention to the teacher's role in classroom interaction and learning. In concentrating on students' classroom interaction, we have tried to shed light upon the significant role of such interaction in supporting and mediating social learning in the classroom. Although we have not explicitly elaborated the teacher's role in student-centred learning, the valuable role of the teacher as a designer of the learning situations and as a supporter of students' learning and interaction has been implicitly present in all the case studies discussed in this book.

No classroom interaction takes place in a vacuum. Rather, it is embedded in the sociocultural context of an activity, shaped by its practices and participants – both the teacher and students – across time (Wells, 1999). The glimpses of students' classroom interactions that we have illuminated with detailed analyses in this book have been part of learning projects in which the students have participated. Consequently, each setting and activity investigated was embedded within the wider pedagogical practices of the classroom in question. Often, these practices included whole-class teaching before and after small-group activities. In these whole-class interactions, the classroom learning community usually started their investigations around a learning theme with a wider, collective activity. This was followed by more independent activities in small groups. The processes and outcomes of these group activities were then usually discussed and elaborated in whole-class interactions. The role of the teacher was more salient and explicit in the whole-class periods, but the teacher was 'present' in all the learning episodes.

As the case studies presented in this book show, not all student groups will engage in productive, task-focused interactions. The reasons for unproductive interactions are many, being related to, among other things, the nature of the task, the organisation of the group and the students' personal characteristics, including their cognitive and social habits and skills. In the classroom, a teacher is likely to face situations in which it may be necessary to participate in the students' group interactions in order to guide the students onto meaningful learning trajectories. The teacher's skills in monitoring students' group interactions, timing interventions and providing the right level of assistance are highly significant and urgently need further investigation.

Conclusion

Social and economic changes in today's society have compelled educators and researchers to rethink the goals of education in terms of the skills students are likely to need in their future lives. Conventional forms of teaching, in which learners have rather passively received knowledge from the teacher or from other authorised materials (cf. Sfard, 1998), have been found inadequate in supporting the development of students' thinking and learning skills, which need to be applied outside of the school situation, in a society full of complex information and problem solving (Brown, Collins and Duguid, 1989; Resnick, 1989). Furthermore, traditional education has, by and large, been based on the acquisition metaphor, in which emphasis is placed on individual enrichment and cognitive achievements. Minor attention has been paid to the development of the social and socio-emotional skills needed for participation in a multicultural society in an ethically responsible manner (Kovalainen, Kumpulainen and Vasama, in press).

The conventional pedagogical practices of the classroom have recently been challenged by the metaphor of collaborative learning in a community of learners, in which emphasis is placed on collective meaning-making and socially shared expertise (see e.g. Brown, Metz and Campione, 1996; Elbers and Streefland, 2000; Rogoff, 1994). Whereas in the conventional classroom the practice of teaching has mainly consisted of lecturing, explaining and checking on the acquisition of convergent and largely factual knowledge (cf. Tharp and Gallimore, 1988), in classrooms built around communities of learners, the activity of teaching and learning is socially negotiated and constructed through ongoing social interactions (Rogoff, 1994). The collective process of negotiating diverse approaches to, perspectives on and interpretations of a shared understanding is seen as giving learners opportunities to extend their level of participation in the cultural practice in question and, correspondingly, to broaden their ways of knowing and thinking (Wells, 1999).

In addition to the need to develop learners' critical, caring and creative thinking for their future lives, the development of the notion of the community of learners has also largely resulted from the need to make the activity of learning and instruction meaningful and challenging for the learner, so that more value is placed on the learner's natural inquiring mind, curiosity and excitement in learning. This has resulted in the construction of learning situations that are open for negotiation and reflective inquiry (Kaartinen and Kumpulainen, in press). In a community of learners, the teacher's role is defined as a sensitive coach or an expert partner who participates in communal learning by orchestrating and scaffolding classroom interaction towards a shared understanding (Wells, 1999).

As discussed in the first part of this book, the theoretical underpinnings of collaborative learning in classroom communities have been strongly influenced by sociocultural theories of learning. In the sociocultural perspective, language and other semiotic tools are seen to play an important role in the construction of proximal zones for learning, during which socially shared meaning-making engenders new perspectives and possibilities yet to be discovered (Vygotsky, 1962, 1978; Wells, 1999). From this perspective, learning is a social and cultural process that takes place via participation in socially shared activities with more knowledgeable members of a culture (Rogoff and Toma, 1997; Wertsch, Hagström and Kikas, 1995). The process of learning is evidenced by the changing nature of participation in a collective activity, from peripheral to central participation (Lave and Wenger, 1991). Consequently, learning is seen to entail enculturation into the practices, discourses and norms of the community.

Today, collaborative and student-sensitive working modes have become more common in classroom teaching. Classrooms and schools are increasingly viewed as learning communities in which participants actively engage in collaborative meaning-making and construct their knowledge with each other and with the outside world (Brown, 1992). Information and communication technology also has a role to play in facilitating such authentic and communicative practices in learning. The aim of such classrooms will often be explicitly stated as to create learning experiences that are organised in collaborative working modes with open-ended and realistic problems, and which allow students to relate their informal knowledge to more scientific knowledge. In these classrooms, students initiate their own questions, which they then proceed to investigate under the teacher's guidance.

Problem-based activities, such as cross-curricular research projects, are carried out in small groups and are followed by joint reflection and evaluation with the rest of the learning community (Goldman, 1997; Wray, 1995). The educational value of the social and interdisciplinary features of such learning contexts can be seen in the increase of students' on-task activity and in the meaningfulness of learning activities stemming from their connections with students' personal interests and real-world problems. These instructional settings demand new skills not often required or supported in traditional instruction. These skills include research skills and skills of handling information in a range of media (Wray, 1995). In addition, they include teamwork and communication skills (Salomon, 1997).

In this book, we have elaborated research on collaborative learning by reviewing current studies of classroom interaction. Furthermore, through our case studies, we have provided information about the nature and dynamics of students' classroom interaction when working in small groups under various academic tasks. The fine-grained analyses of the students' social interaction illuminate the processes and conditions for meaning-making and knowledge construction in peer interactive groups. Furthermore, they highlight how specific features of the learning tasks, the subject domains in which they are embedded and the usage of physical tools promote different kinds of interaction among students. Moreover, the case studies demonstrate the complex processes of collaborative peer learning in which cognitive, social and socio-emotional elements are intertwined.

The case studies and their pedagogical solutions place a specific value on shared experience, voluntary communication and joint meaning-making. In most of the studies, the students were given the opportunity to take an active role in exploring issues and problems that they find meaningful in relation to their earlier experiences and everyday life. The students were given opportunties to engage in reasoning, questioning, discovering and querying assumptions, hypothesising, generalising, inferring consequences, using and recognising criteria, defining concepts, calling for evidence and judging. From the social viewpoint, the students practised skills in learning to listen to others, giving rational arguments, respecting different views and critically and constructively responding to them as well as encouraging others to take part in collective meaning-making. These practices appear to promote skills in students that seem important for their future lives.

As some of the case studies suggest, working as a member of a collaborative working group on open-ended, student-sensitive tasks, appears to change the character of what counts as knowledge and learning (Elbers and Streefland, 2000). In some of the interactions identified in the case studies, the reproduction of knowledge seemed to be less important. Instead, learning seemed to equate with participation in social practices entailing learning to question, to reason, to contribute to problem solving, to argue and to listen to others. These practices are likely to have the power to help produce individuals capable of transformative thinking and learning in the information society. Yet, as some other findings of the case studies show, not all collaborative interactions in the classroom will automatically lead to meaningful learning activities and experiences. In fact, in some cases classroom interaction may entail deficient or even counterproductive learning processes. These findings give evidence of the ways in which students' accustomed patterns of practice, often reflecting traditional school learning in which value is placed on individual products and achievements, can also be echoed in contemporary classrooms despite efforts towards learning as collaborative practice.

Towards an understanding of classroom interaction and learning in contemporary classrooms

In the field of education research, the recognition of the social and cultural aspects of cognition have resulted in an increased focus on the practices, processes and conditions leading to the social construction of knowledge in contemporary classrooms. Understanding reasoning and meaning-making processes in classroom interaction is seen as requiring attention to be given to the evolving social interactions among classroom members as well as to the role of the teacher in scaffolding students' learning together with upholding academic standards and requirements (Hogan, Nastasi and Pressley, 2000). These changes in emphasis have brought with them fresh methodological questions concerning the analysis of classroom interaction. Questions to which researchers have begun to try to find answers include:

- How can the qualitative features in classroom interactions characteristic of a range of learning contexts and classroom cultures be revealed?
- Against which criteria should judgements about the effectiveness of these learning interactions be made?
- How are the various potential characteristics of classroom interaction related to their effectiveness in terms of student learning?

It is clear that this recent focus has challenged the methodological approaches used in the past to investigate collaborative classroom interactions and learning processes, and it seems evident that the methodological tools developed should take a more dynamic and process-oriented approach to classroom interaction and collaborative learning. In addition, they should recognise the role of physical and psychological tools in shaping the nature of collaborative learning activities in the classroom. There is an urgent need for multi-layered analyses that support one another and that enable investigations of the relationships between and within the various layers. It is also true that collective meaning-making processes and conditions for its construction may not be identified unless attention is paid to the development of classroom interactions on a moment-by-moment basis across time.

In this book, we have attempted a number of tasks. Firstly, we have outlined the rationale for and the mechanisms of a developing framework for understanding collaborative learning in peer groups. The emergence of the analytic system described here was influenced by a preliminary interest in the diverse roles, operations and meanings of peer interaction in different learning contexts. Secondly, we have, through the case studies presented in the book, demonstrated some of the potential of this analysis system in unpicking the dynamics of student interaction in learning. Thirdly, and perhaps most importantly, we have also reported on the main findings of our research programme so far and their implications for practice and research. In chapter 9 we presented a review of these findings and a discussion of their implications.

The case studies show clearly that students' talk functions differently in different learning contexts: in some cases peer discourse operates as an integral part of students' activity, whereas in some situations this discourse reveals hardly anything about students' cognitive or collaborative activity. It is not enough, therefore, to draw attention only to student talk if the purpose is to study the complex phenomena of students' interactive activity and learning in the classroom. In order to understand the processes of knowledge construction and the patterns of practice in peer interaction, it is important to take into account not only peer discourse but also other interactive actions contributing towards a shared understanding in the social practices of the classroom.

In our studies, we have sought to illuminate the nature of students' classroom interaction under various learning activities, with a special emphasis on the nature of the social learning situation and dynamics of inter-personal processes. In the future, multi-layered analysis systems like our own might also be used to investigate in greater detail the intra-personal and cultural planes in which classroom interactions are embedded (Rogoff, 1998). The intra-personal analyses might include investigating the qualitative nature of students' knowing as a result of working in collaboration with other members of the classroom. In addition, they could concern the student's social and emotional processes and interpretations of the nature of their learning and the learning activities in which they engage. At the inter-personal and cultural levels, future research needs to investigate collaborative meaning-making across domains in order to identify regularities and domain-specific features that support or inhibit successful collaboration and learning, particularly in open-ended learning situations. More attention also needs to be paid to the emergence of conceptual learning in collaborative interaction, and to the conditions under which each student could be provided with the opportunity to participate in collective meaning-making to their full potential. This brings attention onto the role of the teacher as a participant in collaborative learning practices of the classroom, as well as onto the process of constructing a culture of collaboration in the classroom. As these questions demonstrate, we have made, and describe in this book, a start on such ambitious research targets, yet there is much more still to do.

References

Adams, A. (1985). Talking, listening and the microcomputer. In D. Chandler and S. Marcus (Eds.), *Computers and Literacy* (pp. 41–55). Milton Keynes: Open University Press.

Anderson, J. R., Reder, L. M. and Simon, H. A. (1997). Situative versus cognitive perspectives: Form versus substance. *Educational Researcher, 26*(1), 18–21.

Arvaja, M., Häkkinen, P., Eteläpelto, A. and Rasku-Puttonen, H. (2000). Collaborative processes during report writing of a science learning project: The nature of discourse as a function of task requirements. *European Journal of Psychology of Education, XV*, 455–466.

Austin, J. L. (1962). *How to do Things with Words*. Oxford: Clarendon Press.

Azmitia, M. (1996). Peer interactive minds: Developmental, theoretical, and methodological issues. In P. B. Baltes and U. M. Staudinger (Eds.), *Interactive Minds. Life-span Perspectives on the Social Foundation of Cognition* (pp. 133–162). Cambridge: Cambridge University Press.

Azmitia, M. and Montgomery, R. (1993). Friendship, transactive dialogues, and the development of scientific reasoning. *Social Development, 2*, 202–221.

Baker, L. and Brown, A. L. (1984). Cognitive monitoring in reading. In J. Flood (Ed.), *Understanding Reading Comprehension: Cognition, Language, and the Structure of Prose* (pp. 21–44). Newark, DE: International Reading Association.

Bakhtin, M. M. (1986). *Speech Genres and Other Late Essays* (C. Emerson and M. Holquist, Eds., V. McGee, Trans.). Austin: University of Texas Press.

Bales, R. (1951). *Interaction Process of Analysis. A Method for the Study of Small Groups*. Cambridge, MA: Addison Wesley.

Bangert-Drowns, R. (1993). The word processor as an instructional tool: A meta-analysis of word processing in writing instruction. *Review of Educational Research, 63*(1), 69–93.

Barab, S. A., Bowdish, B. E. and Lawless, K. A. (1997). Hypermedia navigation: Profiles of hypermedia users. *Educational Technology Research and Development, 45*, 23–21.

Barnes, D. and Todd, F. (1977). *Communication and Learning in Small Groups*. London: Routledge and Kegan Paul Ltd.

Barnes, D. and Todd, F. (1995). *Communication and Learning Revisited: Making Meaning Through Talk*. Portsmouth, NH: Boynton/Cook Publishers Heinemann.

Bellack, A., Kliebard, H., Hyman, R. and Smith, F. Jr. (Eds.). (1966). *The Language of the Classroom*. New York: Teachers College Press.

Bennett, N. and Dunne, E. (1992) *Managing Classroom Groups*. Hemel Hempstead: Simon and Schuster

Bennett, N., Wood, E. and Rogers, S. (1997) *Teaching Through Play*. Milton Keynes: Open University Press

Bereiter, C. and Scardamalia, M. (1987). *The Psychology of Written Composition*. Hillsdale, NJ: Erlbaum.

Berger, P. L. and Luckmann, T. (1966). *Social Construction of Reality*. New York: Doubleday and Company, Inc.

Berkowitz, M. W., Oser, F. and Althof, W. (1987). The development of sociomoral discourse. In W. M. Kurtines and J. L. Gewirtz (Eds.), *Moral Development Through Social Interaction* (pp. 322–352). New York: Wiley.

Berqvist, K. and Säljö, R. (1995, August). *Social Languages in Classroom Discourse – Identifying and Appropriating Knowledge*. Paper presented at the 6th European Association for Research on Learning and Instruction conference. Nijmegen, the Netherlands.

Blake, Y. (1990). Word-processing with infants. *Micro Scope, 29*, 5–10.

Bransford, J. D., Goldman, S. R. and Vye, N. J. (1991). Making a difference in peoples' abilities to think. Reflections on a decade of work and some hopes for the future. In L. Chakagi and R. J. Sternberg (Eds.), *Directors of Development: Influences on Children* (pp. 147–180). Hillsdale, NJ: Erlbaum.

Brown, A. (1994). The advancement of learning. *Educational Researcher, 23*, 4–12

Brown, A. L. (1992). Design experiments: Theoretical and methodological challenges in creating complex interventions in classroom settings. *Journal of the Learning Sciences, 2*, 141–178.

Brown, A. L. and Campione, J. C. (1990). Communities of learning and thinking, or a context by any other name. *Human Development, 21*, 108–125.

Brown, A. L. and Palincsar, A. S. (1989). Guided co-operative learning and individual knowledge acquisition. In L. B. Resnick (Ed.), *Knowing, Learning, and Instruction: Essays in Honor of R. Glaser* (pp. 393–451). Hillsdale, NJ: Erlbaum.

Brown, A. L., Armbruster, B. and Baker, L. (1986). The role of metacognition in reading and studying. In J. Orasanu (Ed.), *Reading Comprehension: From Research to Practice* (pp. 49–75). London: Lawrence Erlbaum.

Brown, A. L., Metz, K. E. and Campione, J. C. (1996). Social interaction and individual understanding in a community of learners: The influence of Piaget and Vygotsky. In A. Tryphon and J. Vonèche (Eds.), *Piaget –*

Vygotsky, *The Social Genesis of Thought* (pp. 145–170). Hove: Psychology Press.

Brown, G. and Yule, G. (1983). *Discourse Analysis*. Cambridge: Cambridge University Press.

Brown, J. S., Collins, A. and Duguid, P. (1989). Situated cognition and the culture of learning. *Educational Researcher, 18*, 32–42.

Brown, R. A. J. and Renshaw, P. D. (1996). Collective argumentation in the primary mathematics classroom: Towards a community of practice. In P. C. Clarkson (Ed.), *Technology in Mathematics Education: Proceedings of the Nineteenth Annual Conference of the Mathematics Education Research Group of Australia* (MERGA) (pp. 85–92). Melbourne: Mathematics Education Research Group of Australia.

Brown, R. A. J. and Renshaw, P. D. (2000). Collective Argumentation: A socio-cultural approach to reframing classroom teaching and learning. In H. Cowie and G. van der Aalsvoort (Eds.), *Social Interaction in Learning and Instruction. The Meaning of Discourse for the Construction of Knowledge* (pp. 52–66). Amsterdam: Pergamon Press.

Bruner, J. (1990). *Acts of Meaning*. Cambridge, MA: Harvard University Press.

Butterworth, G. and Light, P. (Eds.). (1992). *Context and Cognition: Ways of Learning and Knowing*. Hertfordshire: Simon and Schuster.

Campbell, D. (1988). A case-study of computer aided writing in a primary school. *Micro Scope Special*, 9–18.

Cazden, C. (1986) 'Classroom discourse', in Wittrock, M. (Ed.), *Handbook of Research on Teaching* (3rd edition) New York: Macmillan.

Cazden, C. (1988). *Classroom Discourse: The Language of Teaching and Learning*. Portsmouth, NH: Heinemann Educational Books Inc.

Champagne, A. (1992). Cognitive research on thinking in academic science and mathematics: Implications for practice and policy. In D. F. Halpern (Ed.), *Enhancing Thinking Skills in the Sciences and Mathematics* (pp. 117–133). Hillsdale, NJ: Erlbaum.

Chandler, D. (1990). The educational ideology of the computer. *British Journal of Educational Technology, 21*(3), 164–174.

Charney, D. (1987). Comprehending non-linear text: The role of discourse cues and reading strategies. In J. Smith and F. Halasz (Eds.), *Hypertext '87 Proceedings* (pp. 109–120). New York: Association for Computing Machinery.

Cobb, P. (1994). Where is the mind? Constructivist and sociocultural perspectives on mathematical development. *Educational Researcher, 23*(7), 13–20.

Cochran-Smith, M. (1991). Word processing and writing in elementary classrooms: A critical review of related literature. *Review of Educational Research, 6*(1), 107–155.

Cohen, E. (1994). Restructuring the classroom: Conditions for productive small groups. *Review of Educational Research, 64*(1), 1–35.

Cole, M. (1996). *Culture in Mind*. Cambridge, MA: Harvard University Press.

Cowie, H. and van der Aalsvoort, G. (Eds.). (2000). *Social Interaction in Learning and Instruction. The Meaning of Discourse for the Construction of Knowledge.* Amsterdam: Pergamon Press.

Crook, C. (1994). *Computers and Collaborative Experience of Learning.* London: Routledge.

Daiute, C. (1985). *Writing and Computers.* Reading: Addison-Wesley.

Daiute, C. (1986). Physical and cognitive factors in revising: Insights from studies with computers. *Research in the Teaching of English, 20,* 141–159.

Davies, G. (1989). Writing without a pencil. In M. Styles (Ed.), *Collaboration and Writing* (pp. 93–105). Milton Keynes: Open University Press.

Davydov, V. V. (1995). The influence of L. S. Vygotsky on education theory, research, and practice. *Educational Researcher, 24*(3), 12–21.

DeCorte, E. (1990). Learning with new information technologies in schools: Perspectives from the psychology of learning and instruction. *Journal of Computer Assisted Learning, 6,* 69–87.

Delamont, S. (1976). *Interaction in the classroom: Contemporary sociology of the school.* Suffolk: Richard Clay Ltd.

Department of Education and Science (DES) (1975). *A Language for Life.* London: HMSO.

DeVries, R. (1997). Piaget's social theory. *Educational Researcher, 26*(2), 4–17.

Dickinson, D. (1986). Cooperation, collaboration, and a computer: Integrating a computer into a first-second grade writing program. *Research in the Teaching of English, 20*(4), 357–378.

Dillenbourg, P. (1999). (Ed.) *Collaborative Learning: Cognitive and Computational Approaches.* Amsterdam: Pergamon Press.

Doise, W. and Mugny, G. (1984). *The Social Development of the Intellect.* Oxford: Pergamon Press.

Dorling Kindersley (1996). *Encyclopaedia of Science.* London: Dorling Kindersley.

Downey, M. and Kelly, A. (1979). *Theory and Practice of Education: An Introduction.* London: Harper and Row.

Dunkin, M. and Biddle, B. (1974). *The Study of Teaching.* New York: Holt, Rinehart and Winston.

Edwards, A. and Furlong, V. (1978) *The Language of Teaching.* London: Heinemann Educational.

Edwards, A. and Westgate, D. (1987). *Investigating Classroom Talk.* London: Falmer Press.

Edwards, A. and Westgate, D. (1994). *Investigating Classroom Talk* (2nd ed.). Basingstoke: Falmer Press.

Edwards, D. (1993). Concepts, memory, and the organization of pedagogic discourse: A case study. *Educational Research, 19,* 205–225.

Edwards, D. and Mercer, N. (1987). *Common Knowledge: The Development of Understanding in the Classroom.* London: Methuen.

Edwards, D. and Potter, J. (1992). *Discursive Psychology.* Newbury Park, CA: Sage.

Elbers, E. and Streefland, L. (2000). 'Shall we be researchers again?' Identity and social interaction in a community of inquiry. In H. Cowie and G. van der Aalsvoort (Eds.), *Social Interaction in Learning and Instruction: The Meaning of Discourse for the Construction of Knowledge* (pp. 35–51). Amsterdam: Pergamon Press.

Englert, C. S. (1992). Writing instruction from a sociocultural perspective: The holistic, dialogic and social enterprise of writing. *Journal of Learning Disabilities, 25,* 153–172.

Feldman, C. (1990). Thought from language: the linguistic construction of cognitive representations. In J. Bruner and H. Haste (Eds.), *Making Sense. The Child's Construction of the World* (pp. 131–146). London: Routledge.

Fisher, E. (1993). Distinctive features of pupil–pupil classroom talk and their relationship to learning: How discursive exploration might be encouraged. *Language and Education, 7,* 239–257.

Fisher, E. (1996). Identifying effective educational talk. *Language and Education, 10,* 237–253.

Flanders, N. (1970). *Analysing Teacher Behaviour.* New York: Addison Wesley

Fleer, M. (1992). Identifying teacher–child interaction which scaffolds scientific thinking in young children. *Science Education, 76,* 373–397.

Foltz, P.W. (1996). Comprehension, coherence, and strategies in hypertext and linear text. In J-F. Rouet, J. J. Levonen, A. Dillon and R. J. Spiro (Eds.), *Hypertext and Cognition* (pp. 109–136). Mahwah, New Jersey: Lawrence Erlbaum Associates.

Forman, E. (1989). The role of peer interaction in the social construction of mathematical knowledge. *International Journal of Educational Research, 13,* 55–70.

Forman, E. and Cazden, C. (1985). The cognitive value of peer interaction. In J. Wertsch, (Ed.), *Culture, Communication and Cognition: Vygotskian Perspectives.* New York: Cambridge University Press.

Fourlas, G. (1988). A comparative study of the functions of children's oral language in teacher-centred and peer-group centred methods of teaching in Greek primary schools. Unpublished M.Ed. thesis. University College, Cardiff.

Fourlas, G. and Wray, D. (1990). Children's oral language: A comparison of two classroom organisational systems. In D. Wray (Ed.), *Emerging Partnerships: Current Research in Language and Literacy* (pp. 76–86). Clevedon: Multilingual Matters Ltd.

French, P. (1987). Language in the primary classroom. In S. Delamont (Ed.), *The Primary School Teacher.* London: Falmer Press.

Fuchs, L. S., Fuchs, D., Karns, K., Hamlett, C. L., Dutka, S. and Katzaroff, M. (1996). The relation between student ability and the quality and effectiveness of explanations. *American Educational Research Journal, 33,* 631–664.

Fuchs, L. S., Fuchs, D., Kazdan, S., Karns, K., Calhoon, M., Hamlett, C. and Hewlett, S. (2000). Effects of workgroup structure and size on student productivity during collaborative work on complex tasks. *The Elementary School Journal, 100,* 183–212.

Galton, M., Simon, B. and Croll, P. (1980). *Inside the Primary Classroom.* London: Routledge and Kegan Paul.

Garner, R., Alexander, P. A., Gillingham, M. G., Kulikowich, J. M. and Brown, R. (1991). Interest and learning from text. *American Educational Research Journal, 28,* 643–660.

Gay, G. and Mazur, J. (1993). The utility of computer tracking tools for user-centred design. *Educational Technology, 33,* 45–59.

Goldman, S. R. (1996). Reading, writing, and learning in hypermedia environments. In H. Van Oostendorp and S. de Mul (Eds.), *Cognitive Aspects of Electronic Text Processing* (pp. 7–42). Norwood, NJ: Ablex Publishing Corporation.

Goldman, S. R. (1997). Learning from text: Reflections on the past and suggestions for the future. *Discourse Processes, 23,* 357–398.

Graesser, A. C. and Person, N. K. (1994). Question asking during tutoring. *American Educational Research Journal, 31,* 104–137.

Green, J. and Mayer, L. (1991). The embeddedness of reading in classrom life: Reading as a situated process. In C. Baker and A. Luke (Eds.), *Toward a Critical Sociology of Reading Pedagogy* (pp. 141–160). Amsterdam: Benjamins Publishing Company.

Green, J. and Wallat, C. (1981). Mapping instructional conversations – a sociolinguistic ethnography. In J. Green and C. Wallat (Eds.), *Ethnography and Language in Educational Settings* (pp. 161–228). Norwood, NJ: Ablex Publishing Corporation.

Greeno, J. G. (1997). On claims that answer the wrong questions. *Educational Researcher, 26,* 5–17.

Grossen, M. (1994). Theoretical and methodological consequences of a change in the unit of analysis for the study of peer interactions in a problem solving situation. *European Journal of Psychology of Education, 11,* 159–173.

Haas, C. and Hayes, J. (1986). What did I just say? Reading problems in writing with the machine. *Research in the Teaching of English, 20*(1), 22–35.

Halliday, M. (1975). *Learning How to Mean.* London: Edward Arnold.

Halliday, M. A. K. and Hasan, R. (1989). *Language, Context, and Text.* London: Oxford University Press.

Hammond, N. (1993). Learning with hypertext: Problems, principles and prospects. In C. McKnight, A. Dillon and J. Richardson (Eds.), *Hypertext: a Psychological Perspective* (pp. 51–69). New York: Ellis Horwood.

Hawisher, G. E. (1986). The effects of word processing on the revision strategies of college freshmen. *Research in the Teaching of English, 21,* 145–159.

Hawisher, G. E. (1989). Research update: Writing and word processing. *Computers and Compositon, 5*(2), 7–27.

Hicks, D. (1995). Discourse, learning and teaching. In M. W. Apple (Ed.), *Review of Research in Education* (pp. 49–95). Washington, DC: American Educational Research Association.

High, J. and Fox, C. (1984). Seven year olds discover microwriters – Implications for literacy of autonomous and collaborative learning in the infant classroom. *English in Education, 18*(2), 15–25.

Hill, J. R. and Hannafin, M. J. (1997). Cognitive strategies and learning from the world wide web. *Educational Technology Research and Development, 45*, 37–64.

Hogan, K., Nastasi, B. K. and Pressley, M. (2000). Discourse patterns and collaborative scientific reasoning in peer and teacher-guided discussions. *Cognition and Instruction, 17*, 379–432.

Hoogsteder, M., Maier, R. and Elbers, E. (1996). The architecture of adult–child interaction. Joint problem solving and the structure of cooperation. *Learning and Instruction, 6*(4), 345–358.

Jackson, B., Fletcher, B. and Messer, D. (1992). When talking doesn't help: An investigation of microcomputer group problem solving. *Learning and Instruction, 2*(3), 185–197.

Jennings, L. B. and Green, J. L. (Eds.). (1999). Locating Democratic and transformative practices in classroom discourse. *Journal of Classroom Interaction, 34*(2).

Joiner, R., Messer, D., Light, P. and Littleton, K. (1995, August). *Investigating the Relationship Between Communicative Style and Productive Interaction.* Paper presented at the 6th European Conference for Research on Learning and Instruction, Nijmegen, the Netherlands.

Jonassen, D. H. and Wang, S. (1993). Acquiring structural knowledge from semantically structured hypertext. *Journal of Computer-Based Instruction, 20*, 1–8.

Jonassen, D. H., Beissner, K. and Yacci, M. (1993). *Structural Knowledge: Techniques for Representing, Conveying, and Acquiring Structural Knowledge.* Hillsdale, NJ: Erlbaum.

Kaartinen, S. (1995). *Konstruktivismi luonnontieteiden oppimisessa. Yhteistoiminta arkitiedon ja tieteellisen tiedon yhteensovittamisessa vaikuttavissa kysymyksissä* [Constructivism in learning science. Constructing collaboration between real life knowledge and scientific knowledge]. Unpublished licentiate thesis. University of Oulu, Finland.

Kaartinen, S. and Kumpulainen, K. (in press). Collaborative inquiry and the construction of explanations in the learning of science. *Learning and Instruction.*

Kahn, J. (1988). Learning to write with a new tool: A study of emergent writers using word processing. Unpublished Doctoral dissertation, University of Pennsylvania, USA.

Keith, G. and Glover, M. (1987). *Primary Language Learning with Microcomputers.* Beckenham: Croom Helm Ltd.

King, A. (1989). Verbal interaction and problem-solving within computer assisted cooperative learning groups. *Educational Computing Research*, 5(1), 1–15.

King, A. (1992). Facilitating elaborative learning through guided student-generated questioning. *Educational Psychologist, 27*, 111–126.

Konttinen, R. (1985). Työvälineorientaatio ja työvälineohjelmien käyttö äidinkielen opetuksessa [Tool-orientation and computers in the teaching of first language]. In R. Konttinen (Ed.), *Työvälineohjelmat äidinkielen opetuksessa* (pp. 7–32). Kasvatustieteiden Tutkimuslaitos, Jyväskylän Yliopisto, Jyväskylä: Kirjapaino Kari Ky.

Koskinen, I. (1990). *Computers and Mother-tongue Teachers* (Research Report No. 91). Department of Teacher Education, University of Helsinki, Finland.

Kovalainen, H., Kumpulainen, K. and Vasama, S. (in press). Orchestrating classroom interaction in a community of inquiry. *Journal of Classroom Interaction*.

Kruger, A. C. (1993). Peer collaboration: Conflict, cooperation, or both? *Social Development, 2*, 165–183.

Kumpulainen, K. (1994). The nature of children's oral language interactions during collaborative writing experience at the computer. (Unpublished doctoral dissertation). Exeter: University of Exeter.

Kumpulainen, K. (1996). The nature of peer interaction in the social context created by the use of word processors. *Learning and Instruction, 6*, 243–261.

Kumpulainen, K. and Mutanen, M. (1998). Collaborative practice of science construction in a computer-based multimedia environment. *Computers and Education, 30*, 75–85.

Kumpulainen, K. and Mutanen, M. (1999). Interaktiotutkimus sosiokulturaalisen ja konstruktivistisen oppimisnäkemyksen viitekehyksessä. [Social interaction and learning – Interaction research within the framework of sociocultural and constructivist perspectives to learning]. *Kasvatus, Finnish Journal of Educational Research, 1*, 5–17

Langer, J. A. and Applebee, A. N. (1986). Reading and writing instruction: Toward a theory of teaching and learning. In E. Z. Rothkopf (Ed.), *Review of Research in Education* (Vol. 13, pp. 171–194). Washington, DC: American Educational Research Association.

Lave, J. and Wenger, E. (1991). *Situated Learning. Legitimate Peripheral Participation*. Cambridge: Cambridge University Press.

Lawless, K. L. and Brown, S. W. (1997). Multimedia learning environments: Issues of learner control and navigation. *Instructional Science, 25*, 117–131.

Lehtinen, E. (1997). Tietoyhteiskunnan haasteet ja mahdollisuudet oppimiselle. In E. Lehtinen (Ed.), *Verkkopedagogiikka* (pp. 12–40). Helsinki: Edita.

Lemke, J. L. (1990). *Talking Science: Language, Learning and Values*. Norwood, NJ: Ablex Publishing Corporation.

Leontjev, A. N. (1981). *Problems of the Development of the Mind*. Moscow: Progress Publishers.

Light, P. and Blaye, A. (1990). Computer based learning: The social dimensions. In H. Foot, M. Morgan and R. Shute (Eds.), *Children Helping Children* (pp. 135–137). Chichester: Wiley.

Light, P., Foot, T., Colbourn, C. and McClelland, I. (1987). Collaborative interactions at the microcomputer keyboard. *Educational Psychology, 7*, 13–21.

Light, P., Littleton, K., Messer, D. and Joiner, R. (1994). Social and communicative processes in computer-based problem solving. *European Journal of Psychology of Education, 14*(1), 93–109.

Littleton, K. and Light, P. (Eds.). (1999). *Learning with Computers. Analysing Productive Interaction.* London: Routledge.

MacArthur, C. and Graham, S. (1987). Learning disabled students' composing under three methods of text production: handwriting, word processing and dictation. *Journal of Special Education, 21*, 22–24.

McGilly, K. (Ed.). (1994). *Classroom Lessons: Integrating Cognitive Theory and Classroom Practice.* London: MIT Press.

McMahon, H. (1990). Collaborating with computers. *Journal of Computer Assisted Learning, 6*(3), 149–167.

Maybin, J. (1991). Children's informal talk and the construction of meaning. *English in Education, 25*, 34–49.

Mead, G. H. (1934). *Mind, Self and Society. From the Standpoint of Social Behaviorist.* Chicago: University of Chicago Press.

Megarry, J. (1988). Hypertext and computer discs: The challenge of multimedia learning. *British Journal of Educational Technology, 19*, 172–183.

Mehan, H. (1979). *Learning Lessons: Social Organization in the Classroom.* Cambridge, MA: Harvard University Press.

Mercer, N. (1994). The quality of talk in children's joint activity at the computer. *Journal of Computer Assisted Learning, 10*, 24–32.

Mercer, N. (1995). *The Guided Construction of Knowledge: Talk Among Teachers and Learners.* Clevedon: Multilingual Matters.

Mercer, N. (1996). The quality of talk in children's collaborative activity in the classroom. *Learning and Instruction, 6*, 359–377.

Mercer, N. (2000). (Ed) *Words and Minds.* London: Routledge.

Mercer, N. and Wegeriff, R. (1999). Is 'exploratory talk' productive talk? In K. Littleton and P. Light (Eds.), *Learning with Computers. Analysing Productive Interaction* (pp. 79–101). London: Routledge.

Mercer, N., Phillips, T. and Somekh, B. (1991). Research Note, Spoken Language and New Technology (SLANT). *Journal of Computer Assisted Learning, 7*, 195–202.

Miller, M. (1987). Argumentation and cognition. In M. Hickman (Ed.), *Social and Functional Approaches to Language and Thought* (pp. 225–249). London: Academic Press.

Moschkovich, J. N. (1996). Moving up and getting steeper: Negotiating shared descriptions of linear graphs. *The Journal of the Learning Sciences, 5*(3), 239–277.

Nastasi, B. and Clements, D. (1992). Social-cognitive behaviors and higher-order thinking in educational computer environments. *Learning and Instruction*, 2(3), 215–237.

Nastasi, B. K., Clements, D. H. and Battista, M. T. (1990). Social-cognitive interactions, motivation, and cognitive growth in Logo programming and CAI problem-solving environments. *Journal of Educational Psychology*, 82, 150–158.

Newman, D., Griffin, P. and Cole, M. (1989). *The Construction Zone: Working for Cognitive Change in School*. Cambridge: Cambridge University Press.

O'Connor, M. C. (1998). Can we trace the 'efficacy of social constructivism'?. *Review of Research in Education*, 23, 25–71.

Oliver, R. and Oliver, H. (1996). Information access and retrieval with hypermedia information systems. *British Journal of Educational Technology*, 27, 33–44.

Orsolini, M. and Pontecorvo, C. (1992). Children's talk in classroom discussions. *Cognition and Instruction*, 9(2), 113–136.

Palincsar, A. S. (1986). The role of dialogue in providing scaffolded instruction. *Educational Psychologist*, 21, 73–98.

Palincsar, A. S. and Brown, A. L. (1984). The reciprocal teaching of comprehension monitoring activities. *Cognition and Instruction*, 1, 117–175.

Paris, S. G. and Turner, J. C. (1994) 'Situated motivation.' In Pintrich, P., Brown, D. and Weinstein, C. (Eds.), *Student Motivation, Cognition and Learning: Essays in Honor of Wilbert, J. McKeachie*, pp. 213–237. Hillsdale, N.J.: Erlbaum.

Peacock, M. and Breese, C. (1990). Pupils with portable writing machines. *Educational Review*, 42(1), 41–56.

Pearson, H. and Wilkinson, A. (1986). The use of the word processor in assisting children's writing development. *Educational Review*, 38(2), 169–187.

Perret-Clermont, A-N., Perret, J-F. and Bell, N. (1991). The social construction of meaning and cognitive activity in elementary school children. In L. B. Resnick, J. M. Levine and S. D. Teasley (Eds.), *Perspectives on Socially Shared Cognition* (pp. 41–62). Washington, DC: American Psychological Association.

Perzylo, L. (1993). The application of multimedia CD-ROMs in schools. *British Journal of Educational Technology*, 24, 191–197.

Peterson, P. L., Wilkinson, L. C., Spinelli, F. and Swing, S. (1984). Merging the process-product and sociolinguistic paradigms. Research on small group processes. In P. L. Peterson, L. C. Wilkinson and M. Hallinan (Eds.), *The Social Context Instruction: Group Organization and Group Processes* (pp. 126–152). New York: Academic Press.

Phelan, P., Davidson, A. L. and Cao, H. T. (1991). Students' multiple worlds: Negotiating the boundaries of family, peer, and school cultures. *Anthropology and Education Quarterly*, 22, 224–250.

Phillips, T. (1985). Beyond lip-service: Discourse development after the age of nine. In G. Wells and J. Nicholls (Eds.), *Language and Learning: An Interactional Perspective*. London: Falmer Press.

Phillips, T. (1990). Structuring context for exploratory talk. In D. Wray (Ed.), *Talking and Listening* (pp. 60–72). Leamington Spa: Scholastic.

Piaget, J. (1954). *The Construction of Reality in the Child*. New York: Basic Books.

Piolat, A. (1991). Effects of word processing on text revision. *Language and Education*, 5(4), 255–269.

Pressley, M. and McCormick, C. B. (1995). *Advanced Educational Psychology for Educators, Researchers and Policymakers*. New York: Harper Collins College Publishers.

Repman, J. (1993). Collaborative, computer-based learning: Cognitive and affective outcomes. *Journal of Educational Computing Research*, 9(2), 149–163.

Resnick, L. B. (Ed.). (1989). *Knowing, Learning, and Instruction: Essays in Honour of Robert Glaser*. Hillsdale, NJ: Erlbaum.

Resnick, L. B. (1991). Shared cognition: Thinking as social practice. In L. B. Resnick, J. M. Levine and S. D. Teasley (Eds.), *Perspectives on Socially Shared Cognition* (pp. 1–20). Washington, DC: American Psychological Association.

Resnick, L. B., Levine, J. M. and Teasley, S. D. (Eds.). (1991). *Perspectives on Socially Shared Cognition*. Washington, DC: American Psychological Association.

Rogoff, B. (1990). *Apprenticeship in Thinking: Cognitive Development in Social Context*. New York: Oxford University Press.

Rogoff, B. (1994). Developing understanding of the idea of communities of learners. *Mind, Culture and Activity*, 1, 209–229.

Rogoff, B. (1998). Cognition as a collaborative process. In W. Damon, D. Kuhn and R. S. Siegler (Eds.), *Handbook of Child Psychology* (Vol. 2, pp. 679–744). New York: Wiley.

Rogoff, B. and Toma, C. (1997). Shared thinking: Community and institutional variations. *Discourse Processes*, 23, 471–497.

Rommetveit, R. (1985). Language acquisition as increasing linguistic structuring of exierence and symbolic behavior control. In J.V. Wertsch (Ed.), *Culture, Communication, and Cognition: Vygotskian Perspectives* (pp. 183–204). New York: Cambridge University Press.

Rosenshine, B. R. and Meister, C. (1994). Reciprocal teaching: A review of research. *Review of Educational Research*, 64, 479–530.

Rouet, J-F., Levonen, J. J., Dillon, A. and Spiro, R. J. (Eds.). (1996). *Hypertext and Cognition*. Mahwah, New Jersey: Lawrence Erlbaum Associates.

Salomon, G. (Ed.). (1993). *Distributed Cognitions. Psychological and Educational Considerations*. Cambridge: Cambridge University Press.

Salomon, G. (1997, August). *Novel Constructivist Learning Environments and Novel Technologies: Some Issues to be Concerned With*. Paper presented at the 7th European Conference for Research on Learning and Instruction (EARLI), Athens, Greece.

Sarmavuori, K. (1988). *Prosessikirjoittamiskokeilu Turun Normaalikoulussa* [A study of process writing in Turku university high school] (Äidinkielen Opetustieteen Seuran Tutkimuksia 1). Helsinki: Yliopistopaino.

Scardamalia, M. and Bereiter, C. (1993). Technologies for knowledge-building discourse. *Communications of the ACM, 36*, 37–41

Scardamalia, M. and Bereiter, C. (1996). Computer Support for knowledge-building communities. In T. Koschmann (Ed.), *CSCL: Theory and Practice of an Emerging Paradigm*. Mahwah, NJ: Lawrence Erlbaum Associates.

Sfard, A. (1998). On two metaphors for learning and the dangers of choosing just one. *Educational Researcher, 27*, 4–13.

Sharan, S. and Shachar, H. (1988). *Language and Learning in the Cooperative Classroom*. New York: Springer-Verlag.

Sharan, S., Shachar, H. and Levine, T. (1999). *The Innovative School: Organization and Instruction*. Westport, CT: Bergin and Garvey (Greenwood).

Sinclair, J. and Coulthard, M. (1975). *Towards an Analysis of Discourse*. London: Oxford University Press.

Spindler, G. A. and Spindler, L. (Eds.). (1955). *Anthropology and Education*. Stanford, CA: Stanford University Press.

Spiro, R. J., Feltovich, P. J., Jacobson, M. J. and Coulson, R. L. (1991). Cognitive flexibility, constructivism, and hypertext: Random access instruction for advanced knowledge acquisition in ill-structured domains. *Educational Technology, 31*, 24–33.

Stevens, R. and Slavin, R. (1995). The cooperative elementary school: Effects on students' achievement, attitudes and social relations. *American Educational Research Journal, 32*, 321–351.

Teasley, S. (1995). The role of talk in children's peer collaborations. *Developmental Psychology, 31*, 207–220.

Tergan, S-O. (1997). Multiple views, contexts, and symbol systems in learning with hypertext/hypermedia: A critical review of research. *Educational Technology, 37*, 5–18.

Tharp, R. and Gallimore, R. (1988). *Rousing Minds to Life*. Cambridge: Cambridge University Press.

Tisher, R. (1987). Student roles. In M. Dunkin (Ed.), *The International Encyclopaedia of Teaching and Teacher Education*. Oxford: Pergamon Press.

Tolmie, A., Howe, C., MacKenzie, M. and Greer, K. (1993). Task design as an influence on dialogue and learning: Primary school work with object flotation. *Social Development, 2*, 183–201.

Tough, J. (1977). *The Development of Meaning: A Study of Children's Use of Language*. London: Allen and Unwin.

Tough, J. (1979) *Talk for Teaching and Learning*. London: Ward Lock Educational.

Tudge, J. (1992). Processes and consequences of peer collaboration. A Vygotskian analysis. *Child Development, 63,* 1364–1379.

Turner, J. and Paris, S. (1995). How literacy tasks influence children's motivation for literacy. *The Reading Teacher, 48*(8), 662–73.

Tuyay, S., Jennings, L. and Dixon, C. (1995). Classroom discourse and opportunities to learn: An ethnographic study of knowledge construction in a bilingual third grade classroom. In Durán, R. (Ed.), *Discourse Processes (literacy among latinos: Focus on school contexts), 19,* 75–110.

van Oostendorp, H. and de Mul, S. (Eds.). (1996). *Cognitive Aspects of Electronic Text Processing.* Norwood, NJ: Ablex Publishing Corporation.

Vinner, S. (1991). The role of definitions in the teaching and learning mathematics. In D. Tall (Ed.), *Advanced Mathematical Thinking* (pp. 65–81). London: Kluwer Academic Publishers.

Vion, R. (1992). *La Communication Verbale. Analyse des Interactions.* Paris: Hachette.

von Glasersfeld, E. (1989). Cognition, construction of knowledge, and teaching. *Synthese, 80,* 121–140.

Vosniadou, S. (1994). From cognitive theory to educational technology. In E. DeCorte and H. Mandl (Eds.), *Technology-based Learning Environments. Psychological and Educational Foundations* (pp. 11–17). NATO ASI Series F: Computer and Science Systems, Vol. 137. New York: Springer.

Vosniadou, S. (1996). Towards a revised cognitive psychology for new advances in learning and instruction. *Learning and Instruction, 6,* 95–109.

Vygotsky, L. S. (1962). *Thought and Language* (E. Hanfmann and G. Vakar, Eds. and Trans.). Cambridge, MA: MIT Press.

Vygotsky, L. S. (1978*). Mind in Society: The Development of Higher Mental Processes* (M. Cole, V. John-Steiner and E. Souberman, Eds.). Cambridge, MA: Harvard University Press.

Webb, N. M. (1991). Task-related verbal interaction and mathematics learning in small groups. *Journal for Research in Mathematics Education, 22,* 366–389.

Webb, N. M. and Farivar, S. (1994). Promoting helping behavior in cooperative groups in middle school mathematics. *American Educational Research Journal, 31,* 369–395.

Webb, N. M., Troper, J. and Fall, J. R. (1995). Constructive activity and learning in collaborative small groups. *Journal of Educational Psychology, 87,* 406–423.

Wells, G. (1981). *Learning Through Interaction.* Cambridge: Cambridge University Press.

Wells, G. (1987). *The Meaning Makers: Children Learning Language and Using Language to Learn.* Porstmouth: Heinemann Educational Books Inc.

Wells, G. (1993) Re-evaluating the IRF sequence: A proposal for the articulation of theories of activity and discourse for the analysis of teaching and learning in the classroom. *Linguistics and Education, 5,* 1–37

Wells, G. (1999). *Dialogic Inquiry. Toward a Sociocultural Practice and Theory of Education.* Cambridge: Cambridge University Press.

Wells, G. and Chang-Wells, G. L. (1992). *Constructing Knowledge Together: Classrooms as Centers of Inquiry and Literacy.* Portsmouth, NH: Heinemann.

Wells, G. and French, P. (1980). *Language in the Transition from Home to School.* Final report to the Nuffield Foundation, University of Bristol.

Wertsch, J. (1985). *Vygotsky and the Social Formation of Mind.* Cambridge, MA: Harvard University Press.

Wertsch, J. (1991). *Voices of the Mind: A Sociocultural Approach to Mediated Action.* Cambridge, MA: Harvard University Press.

Wertsch, J. V., Hagström, F. and Kikas, E. (1995). Voices of thinking and speaking. In L. M. W. Martin, K. Nelson and E. Tobach (Eds.), *Sociocultural Psychology* (pp. 276–290). Cambridge, MA: Cambridge University Press.

Westgate, D. and Hughes, M. (1997). Identifying 'quality' in classroom talk: An enduring research task. *Language and Education, 11*, 125–139.

Wilson, B. G. (Ed.). (1996). *Constructivist Learning Environments: Case Studies in Instructional Design.* Englewood Cliffs, NJ: Educational Technology Publications.

Wood, D., Bruner, J. and Ross, G. (1976). The role of tutoring in problem-solving. *Journal of Child Psychology and Psychiatry, 17*, 89–100.

Wood, D. (1992). Teaching talk. In K. Norman (Ed.), *Thinking Voices: The Work of National Oracy Project.* London: Hodder and Stoughton.

Wray, D. (1995). *Teaching Information Skills Through Project Work.* Sevenoaks: Hodder and Stoughton.

Wright, P. (1993). To jump or not to jump: Strategy selection while reading electronic texts. In C. McKnight, A. Dillon and J. Richardson (Eds.), *Hypertext: A Psychological Perspective* (pp. 137–152). London: Ellis Horwood.

Young, A. C. (1997). Higher-order learning and thinking: What is it and how is it taught? *Educational Technology, 37*, 38–41.

Index